Sketches of the Sixties

VOL. 1.—NO. 1.   SAN FRANCISCO, MAY 28, 1864.   TERMS

CONTENTS:

NEIGHBORHOODS I HAVE MOVED FROM.

BY A HYPOCHONDRIAC.

THE BALLAD OF THE EMEU.

THE COUNTESS DIANA.

[TRANSLATED FROM THE FRENCH OF MARIO UCHARD.]

Page one of the first number of

The Californian

The first two articles are by BRET HARTE

Sketches
of the Sixties

by

BRET HARTE

and

MARK TWAIN

———

Being forgotten material
now collected for the first time from
The Californian
1864-67

AMS PRESS
NEW YORK

Reprinted from the edition of 1927, San Francisco
First AMS EDITION published 1969
Manufactured in the United States of America

LIBRARY OF CONGRESS CATALOGUE NUMBER: 77-92173

AMS PRESS, INC.
New York, N. Y. 10003

Dedicated

TO ALL LOVERS OF BRET HARTE
AND MARK TWAIN

Table of Contents

UNCOLLECTED BRET HARTE MATERIAL

CALIFORNIA SKETCHES

CALIFORNIA CONDENSED NOVELS

ESSAYS AND CRITICISMS

UNCOLLECTED MARK TWAIN MATERIAL

List of Illustrations

Introduction

CALIFORNIA *in the sixties was just beginning to feel the pretentious self-consciousness of youth. She was putting behind her the boisterous, devil-may-care playdays of the gold rush and turning her attention to a more serious future. She was beginning to "settle down" and the process was robbing her of much of her picturesqueness. Long-booted, long-bearded miners no longer caroused through the streets at night, spending riotously the money they had earned by a feverish day's work in the mines. Men no longer lived upon the haphazard hope of making a big "strike"; they began to turn their hands to the more tangible and wiser, but less romantic means of gaining a living. They traded in boots and hats and groceries; these at least were surer than fruitless toil at a claim or the chance of the gambling table.*

It was during this period of transition in 1854 that Bret Harte arrived in California, a youth attracted by the romantic stories that he had heard at home. The colorful extravagance of the mines and the miners appealed to his imagination. Their naiveté, their picturesqueness stirred him, and he came to resent the new materialism that was slowly but implacably pushing the old life out of existence. He gives us an interesting description of San Francisco at this time:

"I do not allude to the brief days of 1849, when it (San Francisco) was a straggling beach of huts and stranded hulks, but to the earlier stage of its development into the metropolis of California. Its first tottering steps in that direction were marked by a distinct gravity and decorum. Even during the period when the revolver settled small private difficulties and Vigilance Committees adjudicated larger public ones, an unmistakable seriousness and respectability was the ruling sign of its governing class. It was not improbable that under the reign of the Committee the lawless and vicious class were more appalled by

the moral spectacle of several thousand black-coated, serious-minded business men in embattled procession than by mere force of arms; and one 'suspect'—a prize-fighter—is known to have committed suicide in his cell after confrontation with his grave and passionless shop-keeping judges. Even that peculiar quality of Californian humor which was apt to mitigate the extravagances of the revolver and the uncertainties of poker had no place in the decorous and responsible utterances of San Francisco. The press was sober, materialistic, practical—when it was not severely admonitory of existing evil; the few smaller papers that indulged in levity were considered libellous and improper. Fancy was displaced by heavy articles on the revenues of the State and inducements to the investment of capital. Local news was under implied censorship which suppressed anything that might tend to discourage timid or cautious capital. Episodes of romantic lawlessness or pathetic incidents of mining life were carefully edited—with the comment that these things belonged to the past, and that life and property were now 'as safe in San Francisco as in New York or London'." [1]

"As each succeeding ocean steamer brought fresh faces from the East, a corresponding change took place in the type and in the manners and morals. When fine clothes appeared upon the streets and men swore less frequently, people began to put locks on their doors and portable property was no longer out at night. As fine houses were built, real estate rose, and the dwellers in the old tents were pushed from the contiguity of their richer brothers. San Francisco saw herself naked, and was ashamed. The old Argonautic brotherhood, with its fierce sincerity, its terrible directness, its pathetic simplicity, was broken up. Some of the members were content to remain in a Circean palace of material and sensuous delight, but the type was transferred to the mountains. . . ." [2]

---

[1] *From Pemberton's "Life of Bret Harte", p. 9.*

[2] *From Bret Harte's Collected Works, vol. II, p. 19. Houghton Mifflin edition.*

San Francisco felt not only a commercial quickening but a cultural one as well. It is true that her first efforts were ephemeral, but they were bound to be abortive in such an atmosphere. Perhaps one of the most brilliant as well as the most precarious of these literary adventures was launched by a young newspaper man, Charles Henry Webb, who left the New York Times to come fortune seeking in California. With the characteristic audacity of youth he conceived the idea of establishing a literary journal in San Francisco and calling it THE CALIFORNIAN. *Years later in reminiscence he said:*

"I was—and am—rather proud of that paper. . . . It was called considerable of a paper—to be published so far away from Boston."

In organizing his staff, Webb asked Bret Harte, who was then working in comparative obscurity as compositor on the Golden Era, to join him. Bret Harte had occasionally slipped an article of his own in the Golden Era, but he was not very well known. When the first issue of THE CALIFORNIAN *was brought out there were two contributions from Bret Harte on the front page; a poem, "The Ballad of the Emeu," and an article, "Neighborhoods I Have Moved From." Both were unsigned because the staff had a quixotic idea that the paper should be purely impersonal, and that any fame should belong to it alone, rather than to any individual. Quite naturally such a scheme was found impractical and the later articles are signed.*

One afternoon shortly after Bret Harte had joined THE CALIFORNIAN, *George Barnes called in the office to introduce a young man who had impressed him. Bret Harte tells the story of his first meeting with Mark Twain:*

"His head was striking. He had the curly hair, the aquiline nose, and even the aquiline eye—an eye so eagle-like that a second lid would not have surprised me—of an unusual and dominant nature. His eyebrows were very thick and bushy. His dress was careless, and his general manner one of supreme indifference to surroundings and circumstances. Barnes introduced him as Mr. Sam Clemens, and remarked that he had

*shown a very unusual talent in a number of newspaper con-
tributions over the signature of 'Mark Twain.' We talked on
different topics, and about a month afterwards Clemens dropped
in upon me again. He had been away in the mining districts
on some newspaper assignment in the meantime. In the course
of the conversation he remarked that the unearthly laziness that
prevailed in the town he had been visiting was beyond anything
in his previous experience. He said the men did nothing all day
long but sit around the bar-room stove, spit, and 'swap lies'.
He spoke in a slow, rather satirical drawl, which was in itself
irresistible. He went on to tell one of those extravagant stories, and
half unconsciously dropped into the lazy tone and manner of
the original narrator. I asked him to tell it again to a friend who
came in, and then asked him to write it out for* THE CALI-
FORNIAN. *He did so, and when published it was an emphatic
success.''* ([1])

*The story was "The Jumping Frog of Calaveras," but in
some curious manner yet to be explained, it did not appear for
the first time in* THE CALIFORNIAN, *but was sent to New York
where it appeared in the last number of the Saturday Press.
Immediately after its publication in New York it was copied
in* THE CALIFORNIAN. *Later when the story was published in
book form, many textual changes were made. The version I am
reprinting is the original, and quite different from the familiar
one.*

On September 2, 1864, Bret Harte became editor of THE
CALIFORNIAN *for a period of three months; and again in
December 9, 1865, until December 30, 1865, when Webb re-
assumed the editorship and kept it until May 5, 1866. After
Webb and Harte and Twain left the journal, it became more
and more anemic and about the end of the year 1867 it passed
out of existence. The wonder is that it lived so long. The environ-
ment was not congenial to such an undertaking. It was a period*

([1]) *From Pemberton's "Life of Bret Harte," p. 73.*

*of commercialism and of war, not of art. Ella Sterling Cummins
in her " Story of the Files" says of* THE CALIFORNIAN:

*" It lived to be three years old and has never died. . . . It
made a strong impression at that time, which continues today.
But not a word can be found in the printed page to tell of its
existence;—it is always in men's memories that it has its abiding
place."* (²)

*It was worthy of an " abiding place" in men's memories for
having launched Bret Harte and Mark Twain upon their brilliant literary careers.*

*Because of the rarity of the journal, many of the early articles
of Bret Harte and Mark Twain have been inaccessible to the
general reader. Miss Elizabeth Webb, daughter of Charles
Henry Webb, founder of the paper, was kind enough to lend
me her father's complete file. In looking through it, I was surprised to find so many forgotten articles among its yellowed
pages, and I thought it important to gather them together in a
form convenient to all lovers of Bret Harte and Mark Twain.*

*I had also in my private collection several articles written
during the sixties which I thought might prove interesting. A
poem, "Lines by an Ex-Schoolmaster" written in 1860, was one
of the earliest things written by Bret Harte. I found it in an old
album and it has never been published in his collected works.*

*The speech, "Woman," by Mark Twain, taken from Marsh's
Manual of Phonetic Shorthand of 1868, was unknown to collectors until 1922 when it was brought to my attention by a friend.
This speech was the second thing written by Mark Twain to
appear in a book, but it was not reprinted until 1910. The
version I am reprinting is different in several respects from the
1910 reprint.*

*Very little is known of the work of Bret Harte and Mark
Twain of the sixties, because the files of the publications for
which they wrote have largely been destroyed. Thinking that*

(²) *From Ella Sterling Cummins' "Story of the Files," p. 141.*

students of the period might be interested, I have added a list of all the articles written by Bret Harte and Mark Twain for THE CALIFORNIAN, *giving their dates of appearance.*

I have taken pleasure in preparing this book for the press, and I think it will prove interesting to all other lovers of Bret Harte and Mark Twain, dealing, as it does, with this early period when the two young authors were striving to make a name for themselves. One of Bret Harte's literary ideals was to create a characteristic western type of literature, and here we have the freshest of their thoughts and impressions, written with the enthusiasm of youth. J. H.

SAN FRANCISCO, *September, 1926.*

Preface to the New Edition

THE *first edition of "Sketches of the Sixties" met with a degree of approval and interest that has encouraged me to print a more complete edition. Shortly after the first printing I found that the Bancroft Library of the University of California had a more complete file of* THE CALIFORNIAN *than the one I had used to prepare the first edition, which, while being unusually complete for so rare a publication, lacked a few numbers. Upon looking through this new file, I found several articles that will greatly add to the interest of the book, and one article in particular that I believe to be a literary discovery in showing the genesis of one of Bret Harte's best known masterpieces.*

Besides the addition of the new material there are a few other changes that should be made. Three articles, "The Cunning of Lunacy," "The Merchant's Books" and "The Banker's Clerk" which I included in the first printing over the signature "F. H." are not in this new edition. When Bret Harte first came to California he was known as Francis Bret Harte, and he often signed his letters "F. B. H." and occasionally "F. H." A few years later he dropped the "Francis" and became known simply as Bret Harte. It was because of this fact that I assumed the sketches signed "F. H." were his, but after further investigation I feel the assumption may have been unwarranted and I am excluding them from this new volume.

These omissions are more than compensated for, however, by the new material which I have been able to include. Several of the articles are reviews and comments about Bret Harte and Mark Twain. One that is typical is an amusing review called, "Mr. Harte Criticised," in which the would-be critic solemnly refutes the charge of plagiarism laid to Harte and commends him for his modesty in copying the masters in his "Condensed Novels." How anyone, even a contemporary critic, could miss the delicious humor of the parodies is a problem. There are also several short notices about Mark Twain that show the affectionate regard Californians felt for him from the beginning of his career.

More important than these are the articles written by Harte himself. The first, "Audiences" is a delightful San Francisco sketch that shows Harte's quiet reflective quality. The second, "A Book for the Times," I did not know to be a Harte item, but I am including it on the authority of the late Mr. Kozlay, who was one of the greatest collectors and admirers of Bret Harte in the country. The third article, "Tailings, Second Notice" is, I believe, a discovery that will prove interesting to anyone interested in Harte's works. To my knowledge it has not been noted by any bibliographer, nor has it been republished.

The circumstances under which it was written are interesting. Bret Harte's first appearance in the book world was not as an author, but as an editor. A Miss Tingley made a collection of verse that had appeared in California publications, and from this collection Harte made selections that he published in a book, "Outcroppings, being selections of California verse" to which he wrote the preface. The book raised a storm of criticism among the friends of the aspiring poets who had not been included, and Harte was roundly berated in some of the book reviews. Instead of taking this abuse seriously, Harte was amused, and he wrote two witty parodies of a typical review of an imaginary book called "Tailings, being rejections of California Verse." These delightfully ridiculous articles must have proved disconcerting to the writers of the offensive reviews.

In the second notice of "Tailings" Harte parodies Tennyson's "Locksley Hall" in a poem called "One Horse Flat" which begins:

> *"*Pard'ner, leave me here a moment; leave me here and go before,*
> *Leave me here, and while you're absent I'll prospect a little more.*"

---

*See page 92.

THE poem on the following pages, written in 1860 when Bret Harte was only twenty-four years old, was first copyrighted by John Howell and printed for him in the San Francisco *Bulletin* in 1913, almost fifty years after it was composed. When the author wrote it in the album of Miss Augusta Atwill, San Francisco belle, and signed it with a flourish, "Frank Bret Harte, 16th September, 1860, Aetat 24 plus," he did not intend it to be a "piece of literature," but a youthful tribute of admiration to a pretty girl. In those early days Bret Harte was chary about signing his literary efforts in full. They were usually unsigned, or a modest "F. H." or "Bret" sufficed. Both Miss Atwill and Bret Harte probably forgot the romantic incident, and the poem remained hidden away until it was found many years later by Miss Atwill's daughter, Augusta Bloomer, when she was looking at her mother's old keepsake book.

Lines by an Ex-schoolmaster.

Oh, lady, I'm the "passive voice,"
The mood subjunctive is my choice
    And grammar's my vocation;
"I am" what I at present show,
My future tense the girl will know
    —Who'll give one conjugation

And when my [way?] finally stays
O'er "oceans seas and gulfs and bays",
    I still may dare to trust her;
For where I turn my eyes, 'tis plain
I'm like the native born of Maine—
    My Capitol's Augusta!

Frank Bret Harte
14th September 1861

aetat 24 +

Lines

BY AN EX-SCHOOLMASTER

Oh, lady, I'm the "passive voice,"
The mood subjunctive is my choice
    And grammar's my vocation;
"I am," what I at present show,
My future tense the girl will know
    Who'll give me conjugation.

And when my fancy finally strays
O'er "Oceans, seas and gulfs and bays,"
    I still may dare to trust her;
For when I turn my eyes, 'tis plain
I'm like the native born of Maine—
    My capital's AUGUSTA!

* * *

What unto thee I can haply tell
The tiniest bird doth sing as well.

Out of his own sweet tuneful throat
In faultless measure and rhythmic note

The waters whisper this song of mine
The zephyrs breathe it in every vine

The rose thou makest thy maiden choice
Hath sung it to thee in a perfumed voice

Then all that many-tongued nature says
Hath spared thy poet his meed of praise.

"H."

*In this poem lies, I believe, the genesis of the poem, "Plain Language from Truthful James," more commonly known as, "The Heathen Chinee," which, five years later, made him famous and brought him an almost unprecedented notoriety here and abroad; a notoriety that Harte did not thoroughly enjoy. He wrote the poem in a spirit of fun when he was editor of The Overland Monthly, but not deeming it worthy of that magazine he gave it to Ambrose Bierce, who was then editing the News Letter. Mr. Bierce recognized its value and unselfishly urged Harte to publish it in The Overland. Harte reluctantly consented and it appeared in The Overland in September, 1870. Almost instantly it became tremendously popular and it was on everyone's lips.
* Pemberton tells an amusing story in connection with Harte's chagrin over the notoriety caused by the poem. Soon after he arrived in London for the first time, a certain Lord of high literary reputation asked him to dine at his house. Harte told a friend, who was to be one of the party, that he should enjoy going if he thought they would not mention "The Heathen Chinee." This friend mentioned to the host what Harte had said and the host, loving a joke, arranged with the guests to talk of nothing but "The Heathen Chinee." At first Harte was perplexed, but he saw the joke and was amused at his own expense.*

I have reprinted "The Heathen Chinee" on pages 94 and 95, following the poem, "One Horse Flat." If one compares the two, their similarity will be seen. I have pointed out that "One Horse Flat" is a parody of Tennyson's "Locksley Hall," and it is interesting to note that "The Heathen Chinee" is also a parody; not of Tennyson, but of Swinburne's "Atlanta in Calydon." Harte said that he chose this poem of Swinburne's because it was in just the meter that a man like Truthful James would not use. A line will show this.

> *"Atlanta, purest of women, whose name is a blessing to speak"*
> *"Yet he played it that day upon William and me in a way I despise."*

---

*The Life of BRET HARTE," T. Edgar Pemberton, page 107.

Of course, the fact alone that both poems are parodies proves nothing, but coupled with many other similarities it is significant.

Then, too, there is a mention of the Chinese question in " One Horse Flat":

> *"And the Chinese on the river kicking up a bloody row."*

The Chinese were just beginning to make themselves felt as a problem when this poem was written. Five years later " The Heathen Chinee" is a more fully developed treatment of the same problem, humorously done. And there is also the similarity of names. The writer's "pard'ner" is William in "One Horse Flat":

> *"And I said, 'My festive William, speak and speak the truth to me:*
> *How it is when I've two aces, that thou always dost have three?' "*

and it is also William or Bill Nye in " The Heathen Chinee":

> *"Yet he played it that day upon William and me in a way I despise"*

Furthermore, the whole situation in each poem is very nearly identical. In "One Horse Flat" William conceals the "bower" in his boot, and in " The Heathen Chinee" it is:

> *" . . . . Nye's sleeve;*
> *Which was stuffed full of aces and bowers,*
> *And the same with intent to deceive."*

In each poem it is, as Harte said, " the old, old story of misplaced confidence and violated trust."

As far as I know this is the earliest of the dialectic Bill Nye series that were so popular. The next one was probably " Society Upon the Stanislaus," which begins:

> *"I reside at Table Mountain, and my name is Truthful James;*
> *I am not up to small deceit or any sinful games;*
> *And I'll tell in simple language what I know about the row*
> *That broke up our Society upon the Stanislow."*

Then came the famous "Heathen Chinee," "Truthful James to the Editor," and "The Late Chinese Outrage," and then "Further Language from Truthful James."

Harte was proud of his dialect poems and stories. One of his earliest literary ideals was to create a characteristic Western American literature. The story of "M'liss" published a few years earlier in * "The Golden Era" was his first attempt in prose to create such a literary type, while the little parody, "One Horse Flat" is in all probability his very first effort to attain the same results.

J. H.

San Francisco, *January, 1927.*

---

*While "M'liss" was published as early as 1863 in "The Golden Era," it was not published separately until 1873, several years after the various volumes of Bret Harte's poems, none of which contained "One Horse Flat" which I am now publishing for the first time sixty-one years after its first printing in The Californian.

Sketches of the Sixties

BRET HARTE

CHAPTER I

𝕺n a 𝕲reat 𝕻ublic 𝕴nstitution

FASCINATION I cannot wholly account for has sometimes impelled me to visit a great public institution in this city, and to gaze upon the nervous, anxious crowd that throng its halls and staircases. This desire was the more remarkable, as the impression invariably left upon me, after each visit, was one of profound and depressing melancholy. But in the present instance I am governed by a sense of duty. A paper mysteriously left in my hand commands me to "appear and attend" before the Court of High Jinks for the city and county of San Francisco, to give evidence on the part of the plaintiff in the case of Richard Noakes *vs*. John Stiles. There is something so appalling and peculiar about this document, in which even my name looks unfamiliar and misspelled, in a space several sizes too large for it, that when I read it to my wife I find it difficult to disabuse her mind of the impression that it is only a preliminary to my immediate trial and incarceration for some capital offence. I cannot recognize nor call up the well-known features of my dear friend Dick Noakes in the sentence, "whereof Richard Noakes is plaintiff," although we have often spoken on this subject, and I have promised to tell all I know about that little stock transaction which brought about this lawsuit. Visiting thus, enpanoplied by the law, he is no longer a concrete individual whom I esteem, but an abstract Noakes, with a claim for justice, before whom I fear and tremble.

If I could only be allowed to tell the story my own way; if I could talk confidentially to the Judge, and relate to him some incidents of Noakes' early career; if I could be allowed to illustrate my story with an anecdote without being told it was irrelevant; if I could quote Rochefoucauld without being checked by the remark that the Court did not wish to hear what Rochefoucauld had said, I feel that I could help Richard. But alas! I know how it will be. My friendship will subject me to suspicion. I shall be asked my name with an emphasis that will suggest my having indulged in a dozen aliases. I shall be openly accused of complicity with Noakes. That largeness of statement which naturally fills the mouth of friendship in a court of law is "flat perjury." Already I feel myself incompetent; but when the day comes, I stand, nervously too soon, in the doorway of the great public institution.

Like all great public institutions its design is consistent with a general idea of private discomfort; that being the manner in which architects, in all ages, have shown the distinction between public and private buildings. Ventilation is effected by exhausted receivers in the chambers and court rooms and through drafts in the halls and passages. The basement story is low, as though crushed by the superincumbent weight of the upper stories, or as if the speeches of counsel and the opinions of bench above were really too much for the building. As I glance through the iron grating to my right, I see a number of miserable men and women listlessly walking about, with head and shoulders bent and bowed as though they were wretched caryatides who supported the tottering fabric of the law overhead. Here they were, true progenitors of those mythical personages, John Doe and Richard Roe. Here were the real foundations of the great public institution; here was nourished the roots of that goodly tree whose earliest leaves were suits, complaints and summonses—whose later blossoms were judgments and executions—but whose final fruits were deceitful as the apples by the Dead Sea shore. But haply my business lies higher up in its branches, and I turn away with a sigh of relief from the spectacle of so much vice and misery.

As I cannot find the Court-room of High Jinks unaided, I venture to ask information of one of those guardians of the law who loiter outside the Police office. He is communicative, but detains me long enough to be able to identify me hereafter, having the opinion, (which obtains with his profession generally, I think), that mankind are, as a class, undetected criminals, against whom there is simply an insufficiency of legal evidence. As I pass the Police Court-room I cannot resist a survey of its noisome recesses—of wonder at the peculiar class of spectators, many of whom seem to be professionally related to the prisoners in the dock—and of admiration of the apathetic official who guards its entrance.

I reach the Court-room of High Jinks at last, and find a case in progress. I see a foreshadowing of my fate in an unhappy witness undergoing a rigid cross-examination, who has sunk from a pinnacle of self-confidence to the lowest depths of self-abasement, who smiles painfully and imploringly at the counsel, contradicts himself and is convicted of a thousand absurdities in the lawyer's skilful manipulation. He looks longingly at the open door as I enter, as if meditating a precipitate flight, but speedily relapses into a very limp state and rubs his perspiring palms together feebly. The cross-examination is resumed. He (the witness) has stated that he has seen the plaintiff a great many times? The witness, with great cheerfulness and some show of confidence, has said so. Has he seen him ten times? Oh, yes! Has he seen him twenty times? Yes. Thirty times? The witness has seen him thirty times. Has he seen him forty times? The witness—very damp about the forehead and imbecile in smile—has seen him forty times. Now, will the witness remember he is on his oath? has he seen the plaintiff *seventy-five* times? The witness, gasping for breath—thinks—no, is certain—he has seen the plaintiff seventy-five times. The counsel would recall to the witness his solemn obligations ere he asks the next question—has the

witness seen the plaintiff in the case of Muff *vs*. Puff ONE HUN-
DRED times? The witness, breaking down, wouldn't like to
say. The counsel wants but one answer: yes or no. No! Then
what does the witness mean by saying he has seen the plaintiff a great many times? The crushed witness makes no
audible reply to this perfectly logical and masterly deduction,
and is mercifully permitted to slink away.

I meet Dick Noakes, but a mysterious gulf seems to have
opened between us since the service of that subpœna. There
is no longer a frank interchange of sentiment. I have been
seriously thinking, aided by the scene just transcribed,
whether the words I heard the defendant in the case of
Noakes *vs*. Stokes, utter, were really those I had given
Noakes to understand, and for which I was subpœnaed.
Might I not have been mistaken? Nay, so worked upon am I
by the diabolical influence of this great public institution,
that I begin to doubt the justice of poor Noakes' claim. Perhaps he sees it in my face; perhaps he would have liked me to
have thrown the doubt in his favor; perhaps in very magna-
nimity he fears I might be betrayed by friendship into mis-
statement—but, whatever he thinks, he conceals. He coldly
tells me he will call me when I am wanted, and turns away. I
walk to the corridor and try to divert my uneasy thoughts by
watching the people collected there, or passing in and out of
the Court-room. It is easy to detect the professional and un-
professional man, the client newly summoned and the experienced litigant, the fresh witness and the old frequenter of the
stand. I am tired of meeting the triumphant leer on the face
of strange suitors when new points are made in their favor,
who in pardonable but unpleasant egotism imagine their suit
observed of all others. I am tired of the bullyragging of witnesses. I lean over the iron railing, and, gazing into the court-
yard below, fall into a reverie.

Imagine night coming on in this place. When the Court-
rooms are deserted, and the porters have swept out the last
scraps of paper torn up by the feverish fingers of anxious

suitors and badgered witnesses; when the key of the Clerk's office is turned upon legal bundles, pigeon-holed and piled away, where John Doe and Richard Roe—those urbane children of the law—are tucked in bed and lie quietly at rest; when a footstep in the passage echoes through all the gloomy rooms and loses itself in the canopy over the Judge's bench; when the sound of wheels die away from without and the cold sea-fog fills the corridors; when the lights are turned off, and only a glimmer straggles into the Court from the basement where Vice and Misery never sleep, and where the festering roots of this deadly Upas tree suck the baleful night dews. At such an hour and in such a place, what is to keep the bodiless spectres of dead-and-gone clients—the wraiths of orphans robbed of their inheritance, the pale shadows of defrauded widows—from thronging these stairways? Why should not the spirits of dead men gather round the closed door of the Probate Court and clamor for that intent which the technicalities of the law have shamefully perverted? Lo! they crowd the staircase, they glide in and out of the passages, they fill the Court-room. Cases, long since decided by honorable and learned Judges in the flesh, are reversed before this shadowy tribunal. They take possession of the Clerk's office and the great books of record rustle with the touch of their unsubstantial fingers. They—

But a voice breaks my phantasy. The case is called and I am wanted. I enter the Court-room. The Clerk repeats the oath in a monotonous voice, and with something of this strange fancy still upon me, I rise to speak the truth, the whole truth, and nothing but the truth.

BRET.

CALIFORNIAN, *September* 10, 1864.

CHAPTER II

On an Extinct Public Institution

EAR the terminus of what is now a great public thoroughfare I sometimes pass a certain square whose freshly painted dwellings show it to have lately undergone that change which practical people call "improvement." Yet so impractical am I, and withal so vagrant and reprehensible in natural impulse, that I cannot resist a vague yearning as I recall the olden time when it was simply a beer-garden—called, I think, a Social Hall—and devoted mainly to unrestrained libation and the Waltz. I recall, too, the memorable Sunday when my youthful feet were arrested on my way to church by strains of secular music, and, how, after a moment's irresolution, I basely thrust my prayer-book into my pocket and entered the fatal enclosure. Here, as a conservator of public morals, I might stop. But I grieve to state that I enjoyed myself thoroughly on that occasion, and that many Sundays after, my thoughts would fondly revert from the sermon to the blissful delights of that beer-garden. No one familiar with the dignified and aristocratic service which always distinguished the dispensation at another public institution will for a moment imagine that there was anything in the sermon to suggest those vulgar memories. It was my own wayward fancy which invested the Rev. Mr. Cream Cheese with a lager-beery atmosphere, transformed the delicate white cambric of his pocket-handkerchief to the folds of a napkin, and made him otherwise appear as a festive and gorgeous head-waiter.

I remember—and offer it somewhat in mitigation of my offence—that a majority of those who attended the Extinct Public Institution were women and children, and that on entering that unhallowed enclosure my eyes fell first upon a baby. It is true that these people were principally foreigners, of a class educated to believe the Sabbath a day of enjoyment, and to whom—being Germans—all music was sacred. But the spectacle of so much happy childhood was a "touch of nature" that seemed to make us "kin," and the appearance of one or two infants at the breast made me overlook the bibulous propensities of their parents. Indeed, those babies were everywhere—toddling on the grass, being extricated from the whirling crinoline of waltzers, impending from their mothers' arms, dabbling their impotent fingers in small lakes of beer on the tables, or choking over their first glass and being violently rapped back again into consciousness and ear-piercing lamentation. There were older children, who ran races on the green and indulged in gymnastic exercise, on the poles and bars, or, repairing to the swing, swung themselves so high that the bright dresses of the little girls, seen through the swaying branches, made them look like gaily-plumed birds. I remember also an extravagance of sash, and a faint flavor of freshly-ironed frocks about those innocents, that were quite remarkable. There were older children, too, of both sexes, who sat in Arcadian simplicity with their arms about each other's waists. There were the laughing Gretchen, and the pensive Marguerite—a trifle rosier and stouter than her typical namesake—with blonde hair and blue eyes, and a gentle and persuasive sweetness of voice that belonged to an older civilization than ours, and often afforded an odd contrast to the tones of my fair countrywomen, which are apt to be somewhat stridulous and self-asserting—perhaps because the ancestors of Gretchen and Marguerite were sometimes yoked to a plough, and their descendants were accustomed to servitude, while my fair compatriots were always independent. However it might be, I remember that Gretchen and Marguerite were very happy in the company of two young fellows with sumach-colored moustaches, and I did not begrudge them that seventh-day's recreation which followed their week of domestic drudgery. There was Young America, also, mingling with the crowd—pliant, adaptive, and good-humored. There likewise the inevitable and gorgeous Snob presented himself—all the more pretentious, uneasy and insincere for being in the presence of ease, sincerity and unpretentiousness. But why should I recall him? The Public Institution is extinct, but has he not survived it? Does he not still pervade society, flitting before us like Mr. Pepper's Ghost—a cheap illusion, a theatrical shadow of the real thing—at church, at the opera, and in the *salon?*

At the further end of the hall, seen dimly through a halo of tobacco smoke, I remember to have observed a portrait, executed in the highest style of German art, representing Schiller—I think—with a few lines underneath, that in their complete unintelligibility and redundancy of Z's and S's, seemed to me to be the natural language of intoxication. I remember, too, that as I gazed at it, the band struck up an irresistible waltz, and the circling couples flew by me. I remember, too, how well they danced—those Germans—how the mazes of their cotillion seemed to be modelled upon the terribly-involved sentences of their own metaphysical writers. I remember, too, that, being influenced by the prevailing beverage and the fascinations of Strauss, I found myself shortly after waltzing with somebody in a white waist and blue skirt, but when or how I was introduced I cannot now recall. As she spoke no English and I no German there was nothing to divert our attention from the serious business of the waltz, and our acquaintance ceased with that set. Blonde-haired and slightly adipose maiden! should thy mild blue eyes ever rest on these pages, accept this assurance that thy slim, serious and sallow-visaged partner is still thy debtor.

Such are my loving and tender reminiscences of this Ex·

tinct Public Institution. If I may believe popular report, a
weird influence still extends over the locality. On warm, star-
lit summer-nights, strains of Von Weber are said to float
lightly and mysteriously upon the air, and mingle with the
grateful perfume of adjacent gardens. The shrill notes of the
piccolo have been heard at such times, even above the whistle
of the San Jose cars. The soil is still damp, as with unabsorbed
heel-taps and overflowing libations; a murky fog like that of
tobacco smoke sometimes encompasses that region, and a
brewery has risen over the locality of hops.

BRET.

CALIFORNIAN, *October* 1, 1864.

CHAPTER III

On the Decay of Professional Begging

A S THE new Benevolent Association has had the effect of withdrawing beggars from the streets, and as Professional Mendicancy bids fair to be presently ranked with the Lost Arts, to preserve some records of this noble branch of industry I have endeavored to recall certain traits and peculiarities of individual members of the order whom I have known, and whose forms I now miss from their accustomed haunts. In so doing, I confess to feeling a certain regret at this decay of Professional Begging, for I hold the theory that mankind are bettered by the occasional spectacle of misery, whether simulated or not, on the same principle that our sympathies are enlarged by the fictitious woes of the Drama, though we know that the actors are insincere. Perhaps I am indiscreet in saying that I have rewarded the artfully dressed and well acted performance of the begging impostor through the same impulse that impelled me to expend a dollar in witnessing the counterfeited sorrows of poor "Triplet" as represented by Charles Wheatleigh. I did not quarrel with the deceit in either case. My coin was given in recognition of the sentiment; the moral responsibility rested with the performer.

The principal figure that I now mourn over as lost forever is one that may have been familiar to many of my readers. It was that of a dark-complexioned, black-eyed, foreign-looking woman, who supported in her arms a sickly baby. As a pathological phenomena the baby was especially interesting, having presented the Hippocratic face and other symptoms

First publication with the above title.—EDITOR.

of immediate dissolution, without change for the past three years. The woman never verbally solicited alms. Her appearance was always mute, mysterious and sudden. She made no other appeal than that which the dramatic tableau of herself and baby suggested, with an outstretched hand and deprecating eye sometimes superadded. She usually stood in my doorway, silent and patient, intimating her presence, if my attention were preoccupied, by a slight cough from her baby, whom I shall always believe had its part to play in this little pantomine, and generally obeyed a secret signal from the maternal hand. It was useless for me to refuse alms, to plead business or effect inattention. She never moved; her position was always taken with an appearance of latent capabilities of endurance and experience in waiting which never failed to impress me with awe and the futility of any hope of escape. There was also something in the reproachful expression of her eye, which plainly said to me, as I bent over my paper, "Go on with your mock sentimentalities and simulated pathos; portray the imaginary sufferings of your bodiless creations, spread your thin web of philosophy, but look you, sir, here is real misery! Here is genuine suffering!" I confess that this artful suggestion usually brought me down. In three minutes after she had thus invested the citadel, I usually surrendered at discretion without a gun having been fired on either side. She received my offering and retired as mutely and mysteriously as she had appeared. Perhaps it was well for me that she did not know her strength. I might have been forced, had this terrible woman been conscious of her real power, to have borrowed money which I could not pay, or have forged a check to purchase immunity from her awful presence. I hardly know if I make myself understood, and yet I am unable to define my meaning more clearly when I say that there was something in her glance which suggested to the person appealed to, when in the presence of others, a certain idea of some individual responsibility for her sufferings, which, while it never failed to affect him with a mingled sense of ludicrousness and terror, always made an impression of unqualified gravity on the minds of the bystanders. As she has disappeared within the last month, I imagine that she has found a home at the San Francisco Benevolent Association—at least, I cannot conceive of any charity, however guarded by wholesome checks or sharp-eyed almoners, that could resist that mute apparition. I should like to go there and inquire about her and also learn if the baby was convalescent or dead, but I am satisfied that she would rise up with a mute and reproachful appeal, so personal in its artful suggestions, that it would end in the Association instantly transferring her to my hands.

My next familiar mendicant was a vendor of printed ballads. These effusions were so stale, atrocious, and unsaleable in their character, that it was easy to detect that hypocrisy, which—in imitation of more ambitious beggary—veiled the real eleemosynary appeal, under the thin pretext of offering an equivalent. This beggar—an aged female in a rusty bonnet—I unconsciously precipitated upon myself in an evil moment. On our first meeting, while distractedly turning over the ballads, I came upon a certain production entitled, I think, "The Fire Zouave," and was struck with the truly patriotic and American manner in which "Zouave" was made to rhyme in different stanzas with "grave, brave, save and glaive." As I purchased it at once, with a gratified expression of countenance, it soon became evident that the act was misconstrued by my poor friend, who, from that moment never ceased to haunt me. Perhaps, in the whole course of her precarious existence, she had never before sold a ballad. My solitary purchase evidently made me, in her eyes, a customer, and in a measure exalted her vocation; so, thereafter, she regularly used to look in at my door, with a chirping confident air, and the question, "Any more songs to-day?" as though it were some necessary article of daily consumption. I never took any more of her songs, although that circumstance did not shake her faith in my literary taste; my abstinence from this exciting mental pabulum being probably ascribed to charitable motives. She was finally absorbed by the S. F. B. A., who have probably made a proper disposition of her effects. She was a little old woman, of Celtic origin, predisposed to melancholy, and looking as if she had read most of her ballads.

My next reminiscence takes the shape of a very seedy individual, who had, for three or four years, been vainly attempting to get back to his relatives in Illinois, where sympathizing friends and a comfortable alms-house awaited him. Only a few dollars, he informed me—the uncontributed remainder of the amount necessary to purchase a steerage ticket—stood in his way. These last few dollars seem to have been most difficult to get—and he had wandered about, a sort of antithetical Flying Dutchman, forever putting to sea, yet never getting away from shore. He was a "'49-er," and had recently been blown up in a tunnel, or had fallen down a shaft, I forget which. This sad incident obliged him to use large quantities of whisky as a liniment, which, he informed me, occasioned the mild fragrance which his garments exhaled. Though belonging to the same class, he was not to be confounded with the unfortunate miner who could not get back to his claim without pecuniary assistance, or the desolate Italian, who hopelessly handed you a document in a foreign language, very much bethumbed and illegible—which, in your ignorance of the tongue, you couldn't help suspiciously feeling might have been a price current—but which you could see was proffered as an excuse for alms. Indeed, whenever any stranger handed me, without speaking, any open document, which bore the marks of having been carried in the greasy lining of a hat, I always felt safe in giving him a quarter and dismissing him without further questioning. I always noticed that these circular letters, when written in the vernacular, were remarkable for their beautiful caligraphy and grammatical inaccuracy, and that they all seem to have been written by the same hand. Perhaps indigence exercises a peculiar and equal effect upon the handwriting.

I recall a few occasional mendicants whose faces were less familiar. One afternoon a most extraordinary Irishman, with a black eye, a bruised hat and other traces of past enjoyment, waited upon me with a pitiful story of destitution and want, and concluded by requesting the usual trifle. I replied, with some severity, that if I gave him a dime he would probably spend it in drink. "Be Gorra! but you're roight—I wad that!" he answered promptly. I was so much taken aback by this unexpected exhibition of frankness that I instantly handed over the dime. It seems that Truth had survived the wreck of his other virtues; he did get drunk, and impelled by a like conscientious sense of duty, exhibited himself to me in that state, a few hours after, to show that my bounty had not been misapplied.

In spite of the peculiar character of these reminiscences, I cannot help feeling a certain regret at the decay of Professional Mendicancy. Perhaps it may be owing to a lingering trace of that youthful superstition which saw in all beggars a possible prince or fairy, and invested their calling with a mysterious awe. Perhaps it may be from a belief that there is something in the old-fashioned alms-giving and actual contact with misery, that is wholesome for both donor and recipient, and that any system which interposes a third party between them is only putting on a thick glove, which, while it preserves us from contagion, absorbs and deadens the kindly pressure of our hand. It is a very pleasant thing to purchase relief from annoyance and the trouble of having to weigh the claims of an afflicted neighbor. As I turn over these printed tickets, which the courtesy of San Francisco Benevolent Association has—by a slight stretch of the imagination in supposing that any sane unfortunate might rashly seek relief from a newspaper office, conveyed to these editorial hands—I cannot help wondering, whether, when in our last extremity we come to draw upon the Immeasurable Bounty, it will be necessary to present a ticket.   BRET.

CALIFORNIAN, *June* 17, 1865.

CHAPTER IV

In the Country

I HAVE been in the country. No matter where. Except in the degrees of discomfort, Nature is pretty much alike all over California. She offers grandeur, sublimity, picturesqueness, and delights in heroic attitudes before the tourist, but of purely pastoral and bucolic comfort she knows nothing. She offers you quantity instead of quality—opulence in place of refinement. The same law she obeys in producing monstrous cabbages and gigantic trees is shown throughout all the details of her landscapes. If she has to make a mountain, it is something stupendous; if a valley, it is a perpendicular chasm of several thousand feet; if she has even to cover a field with flowers, it is done so extravagantly that the odorless blossoms seem to have been furnished by contract, and are scattered without taste or judgment. Her rains are deluges—her droughts are six months long. She projects splendid studies for the artist about as unavailable for practical enjoyment as the painted canvas itself. What she loses in delicacy, she makes up in fibre—whether it be strawberries that look as if they had been arrested on their way to become pineapples, or a field of wild oats, whose every stalk is a miracle of size, but whose general effect is most unpastoral and unmeadowlike. For these reasons, I prefer not to name the spot where I have been ruralizing. It is always safer to be attacked for a general heresy than for a mere doctrinal difference; it is less dangerous to commit treason against the State, than to "go back" on one's native village.

My retreat lay near one of the routes of fashionable Summer travel. Groves of fine sturdy trees surrounded it, which bore a faint resemblance to a plucked apple orchard. The soil at this late season (late for California) seemed to be actively engaged in producing straws for sherry cobblers, and there was a marked similarity between the crop in the barrooms of the waysides hotels and those in the fields beyond. Handsome villas dotted the landscape, and a few pretentious gothic redwood palaces were going up in the vicinity. City people, bearing an unmistakable atmosphere of Montgomery street about them, occasionally made their appearance and insulted Nature with their dapper and artificial smartness. For the country was neither neat nor clean. We have the authority of an American writer and painter that the picturesque never possesses either of these qualities, and it would really seem as if Nature took a malicious pleasure in revenging herself upon these smart folk by powdering their shiny boots with her dust, reddening their faces with her sunshine, and blowing their hair out of curl with her zephyrs. There was something peculiarly Californian in the occasional odd juxtaposition of civilization and barbarism. A ride of only a few miles would bring you to rocky canons, hills clothed with primeval redwoods, and here and there a rude log cabin or frontier shanty. Yet in the midst of this wilderness, a turn in the rough mountain trail brings you suddenly upon a vision of smoothly-shaven faces, pork-pie hats, bright dresses, ribbons and light-colored gloves, in a smark rockaway, drawn by well-groomed horses with shining harness. Perhaps a few yards further on you meet the indigenous oxteam, toiling along with its load of rails, preceded by the teamster, unshaven and unshorn, looking as if he might in time so closely assimilate to his oxen as to change places with them. Such is the influence of civilization, however, that it is the ox team which seems the intruder. The teamster recognizes the fact as he turns out of the way to let you pass. In the struggle with civilization and art, nature and simplicity meekly retire. I remember that one day I was lying on the grass under a tree—to me the simplest form of rural pleasure —when a well-dressed horseman, "cutting across lots," rode close by me. He stared at me for a moment, but his glance conveyed such a sense of the outraged propriety of Montgomery street, that had I been reclining on the sidewalk in front of Wells, Fargo & Co., I do not think I could have felt more keenly the sense of ridiculous exposure. But I braved it through, despite the stranger and even despite the ungrateful conduct of Nature, who employed the interval in projecting caterpillars in my face and filling my pockets with coleopterous insects. I would not advise too free an indulgence in this bucolic practice, as the grassy carpet at this season is worn in places, and contact with the soil is productive of sciatica. As I turned into the main road on my way home, I felt a new and mysterious significance in those sign boards with which the whole country abounds, and which bear the unvarying legend, that while it is so many miles to such a place, it is at the same time so many miles to HEUSTON, HASTINGS & Co. I could not help feeling that this last fact really *was*, as the guide board intended it to be, the most important. In proportion as we approximate Nature and rural felicity we increase our distance from our fashionable clothier.

The natives of this region were of pastoral but reticent habits. The effect of a question upon the rural mind was similar to a blow. After the first stunning effect was over, recovery was followed by the attitude of resistance. As the small roads in that neighborhood led nowhere in particular, and were originally organized by cattle in search of water, travelers were often obliged to fall back upon the population for a knowledge of their whereabouts and for directions for their guidance. When an answer could be extracted from these people, it was usually given in a vague, unsatisfactory manner, which generally led the unfortunate man to ask again at the next house and receive a reply equally mysterious. There were allusions to such land marks as Jones' Mill, Brown's Store and Robinson's Field—local authorities of course utterly unknown to the stranger—and directions as to keeping to the right and turning to the left, which generally brought him to a state of miserable perplexity and confusion.

The country is still, but not pulseless. There is such a vague impression of unseen vitality at work, that the silence of a vast open field has a throbbing intensity which affects the tympanum as palpably as sound, and I do not wonder that Horace—I think it was Horace—spoke of that "dreadful noise of nothing" as being peculiarly rural. I speak of the meridian quiet, of course, and not of those hours of the morning and afternoon given up to vocal exercises of bird and insect. But for genuine repose the rural night is the most sincere. There is such a palpably folding of leafy hands, and such nestling beneath the green coverlid. Then the moon, lifting herself cautiously over the pines that fringe the mountain, looks down with a subdued and timid lustre, as if half afraid of disturbing the sleep of birds and flowers. Then with the whimsical tenderness of her sex, she invests with poetry and loveliness, all that else were harsh, uncouth and rugged. A shingle mansion lately built, and just visible through the trees from my window, she touched here and there with caressing fingers, and straightway the coarse unsightly sham became a palace, whose wooden colonnades were turned to marble, whose broad portico shone without a gleam of sickly paint or staring color. She touched the whitewashed fences beyond, and their glaring freshness was subdued to silvery outlines. Even the dusty road became a shining ribbon. As I have a great temptation here to make the usual allusion to Endymion, without which no description of any moonlit landscape was ever complete, I close somewhat abruptly and leave the slumbers of that gentle shepherd for once undisturbed.   BRET.

CALIFORNIAN, *July 15*, 1865.

CHAPTER V

At the Fair

 S I CANNOT hope to add anything to the fast-increasing literature of the Fair, or indeed to offer any ideas of practical utility concerning it, perhaps I ought to say nothing. The *Bulletin's* daily review has interested me, not only for the care and patience displayed in its details, but for the apparent conscientiousness and genial good humor of its criticisms. Being naturally too indolent and inaccurate to excel in the first two qualities, and perhaps somewhat deficient in the two last, the following may afford the reader some change from the regular notices.

As the central figure of the Fair is the colossal statue of Mr. Lincoln, it challenges the attention of the visitor with a degree of self-assertion which I think quite inconsistent with the natural humility of the original. To be plainer, I fear that the real mistake of the sculptor has not been one of detail or outline, but in his conception of Mr. Lincoln as a *colossal* figure. There is no irreverence in saying that our late President had neither the outward heroic aspect which permits this exaggeration, nor the dominant qualities of mind and character which take exaggeration as their appropriate symbol. Perhaps, had he possessed those godlike attributes which would have found this expression, he would not have been as universally beloved. As a colossal figure, he seems removed from that kindly contact with the people; he is a little too large for the heart, and not quite large enough to fill the brain of most Americans. Artistically, the size is unfortunate. Mr. Lincoln was a tall man, but his height, owing to his peculiar formation of limb, was not a grace—the colossal figure intensifies this defect and gives it the effect of a caricature. We have in this monstrous effigy of our late Chief Magistrate, simply protracted homeliness—uncouthness prolonged to an indefinite extent quite beyond the power of any intrinsic kindliness to transfuse or make picturesque. I say this with no wish to decry the imperfections of the subject, nor with any intention of overlooking the general merits of Mr. Mezzara's details, or the insuperable difficulties which modern costume offers to sculpture. I do not object to his preferring the ordinary every-day dress as more suitable to the simplicity of his subject, but the error of proportion makes a giant in a dress coat hardly a fit object for serious and tender contemplation. His mistake is perhaps the more pardonable in a country where Nature is apt to fall into the same errors, and to produce inordinate squashes, and gigantic cabbages. Not far from the statue will be found pumpkins, beets, apples and pears, quite as exaggerated in outline, and I am willing to believe as inevitably sacrificing delicacy, sweetness, and refinement for coarser fibre and size.

Perhaps because I am not of a mechanical turn of mind, and never constructed anything but a ship, in my boyhood, which had a singular tendency to keel over and continue its voyage bottom upward, I am unduly fascinated by machinery. I usually turn into the room devoted to this purpose immeately on entering the Fair, and amuse myself by watching the revolutions of the fly-wheels, the endless continuity of travelling bands and belts, and in listening to the half-human buzz and clatter of stamps and mills, which always impress me as though—like the Prince in the fairy tale—I had become suddenly alive to the language of inanimate objects. The labor of machinery conveys to the lazy man, like myself, none of that tacit reproach which individual or manual labor always suggests to an idle bystander. There is no spectacle of straining sinews and perspiring brows, which robs honest industry of much of its picturesqueness. There is always a dim, prophetic shadowing of a future time when all work will be done by this myriad-handed geni, and man will slip through life solely by the exercise of volition. But if machinery has neither human frailty nor weakness, it has neither human sympathy nor kindness. Any one of these noiseless, shifting, shiny bands will take you up, without outcry, save your own, without anger, without pity, remorselessly whirl you around yonder revolving barrel, and fling you—a shattered wreck—upon the floor, continuing its endless placid journey without a tremor of remembrance or regret for the life crushed out below it. That smooth, shining piston-rod, whose oiled surface almost invites your hand to linger caressingly upon it, will quietly remove that necessary member from your body, crush its bones to powder, and go on as smoothly and as gently as ever, wiping the stains from its treacherous arm without excitement or compassion. Yet there are always people loitering about, whose carelessness leads you to think that they had "made a covenant" with Behemoth, and that they could disarm this fateful monster.

The picture gallery, in its present condition, I am frank to confess, does not exercise any of this terrible fascination. I am unconscious of any period when I could not have been torn away from it without much struggling and resistance. In the photographs of our familiar acquaintances, which adorn its walls, there is always something that invites criticism. The self-satisfied air which these individuals wear is apt to unconsciously excite our resentment, even though we know the individual to be personally modest and retiring. If the pictures are not good likenesses we are apt to experience an ill-defined feeling that our friend has unwittingly developed under the camera some quality of which we were unconscious —some hidden faculty which we knew not. Of course the photograph has in later years undergone much improvement. The operator, though he deal with sunbeams instead of oil colors, is expected to have some artistic taste. The tendency of most sitters to preternatural stiffness and statuesque attitudes, I am glad to observe, is undergoing correction. They are not allowed to sit with their hands on the backs of chairs—the display of rings which that position offers not being considered now as essential to a good likeness. I could wish that equal good sense would obtain in regard to backgrounds and accessories. I do not see why gentlemen should be required to rest their hands on the fragment of a Corinthian column—a habit I am willing to believe not familiar to them in real life under any circumstances. I am at a loss to understand why the gentleman from San Andreas, whose features and garments are unmistakably American, chooses to have himself represented as standing on a terrace beside the Lake of Como; why Mr. Jones, of Front street, prefers to appear in a business suit on the plains of Arabia, with a palm tree over each shoulder; why I, who am not fond of ancient history, should be obliged to stand in an evening dress, with gloves and cane, just beneath the Acropolis, while a Grecian sunset diffuses its chaste glories generally around my person. The striking sameness of the photographic furniture is another defect that should be remedied; in its present peculiarity most sitters appear to have been originally inhabitants of the same house—many, occupants of the same room. Who does not know that little round table with its cloth drooping in accurate folds—possibly the most impossible piece of furniture extant—on which one-half of San Francisco has leaned its right arm, or read its good book. Who does not know that curtain which always looks out of place; that stone balustrade which always appears on a parlor carpet, as if it were a part of the furniture of a drawing-room; the great arm-chair on which most people lean as they never leaned before and never will again. But this digression bids fair to lead me away from the picture gallery, of which it suddenly occurs to me I have something serious to say.

There are, as is usual, in such exhibitions, many poor pictures, and some abominable drawings by young people of either sex, which good taste, I think, would have ruled out of the collection. But I observe with some concern that they afford a convenient opportunity for many simple-minded young men to air their callow criticism, and to make merry over the feeble efforts of an age and condition from which they themselves, I should judge, have not been long emancipated. I would have these young gentlemen remember that there are some things that it is good taste and true criticism to leave uncriticized, and that, poor as many of these efforts undoubtedly are, they must be endured as long as there are loving parents and doting relations to leaven this otherwise selfish world, and that it may be considered doubtful whether the cheap reputation made by a scurrile jest or disparaging comment is as necessary to the formation of character as that gentlemanliness which respects the weaknesses as well as the virtues of others. Being the other day in the gallery at an unfrequented hour, I came upon a hard-faced woman in that lustreless black which is the symbol of protracted mourning, who was dusting one of the most atrocious pictures I ever saw with a thoughtful care and tenderness that I would not have otherwise thought her capable of. The picture, if I remember rightly, represented a frightful storm at sea which would have proved fatal to any vessel less astonishing than the one which now rode the surges. Huge waves of guava jelly threatened to overwhelm her deck, and large flakes of vermicelli hung heavily on her spars and stately bowsprit. A lee-shore, the more terrible from its being composed apparently of chunks of old iron, threatened the hapless vessel with instant destruction. To add to the danger than environed her, out of an inky curtain to windward, a species of highly vindictive lightning forked—I should rather say, pitchforked—malevolently at three giants who composed the crew. As I was endeavoring to scrutinize the picture with an appearance of interest, the old woman timidly approached me.

"You'll see it here in a much better light, sir."

I turned and took the required position. It certainly was a more favorable light. As I stood beside the black bombazined female and looked at the picture, somehow I thought the bedaubed canvass faded quite away, and a bright young face, which might have resembled the one beside me, before grief, care and anxiety had drawn harsh lines around it, beamed pleasantly out of the frame. Still looking at the picture in this remarkably favorable light, I thought it changed to a long street down which a blithe-faced boy with his drawing book and satchel was passing. Again it changed, but this time it was to the hill beside the sea—where a little headstone struggled out of a mound of flowers. Just then the shadow of some passing visitor fell upon the frame. The black bombazined female noiselessly slipped away, and in turning round, somehow I found I had lost the favorable light, and was gazing only at the wretched daub which had at first excited my merriment.

I had intended to say something about Roger's statuettes and the New England Kitchen, but I find that I have already occupied the space allotted to me, and must defer this irregular notice till next week.   BRET.

CALIFORNIAN, *August* 26, 1865.

CHAPTER VI

Among the Books

I N VISITING a certain public library in this city, I sometimes linger beyond the usual period required for the transaction of my business. This is partly the result of a hesitation to choose from so many volumes of apparently equal interest, and partly from an indistinct idea that the mere propinquity of so much learning and instruction is mysteriously beneficial to the mind. Whether I have been able to make any better choice by reason of this extra time taken for selection, or whether the perusal of title-pages has stimulated me to renewed intellectual vigor, I shall not now discuss. These intervals of recreation have been favorable to certain other observations, some of which I am tempted to transcribe.

Penciling and marginal notation—a prevailing epidemic in all circulating libraries—is not unknown here. Although it rages more violently among a feeble class of romances, and breaks out in an unwholesome eruption all over the leaves of most sentimental works, it is generally confined to short, squab, thick novels, in which the hero is usually a clergyman or doctor, much older than the heroine who undergoes what is termed a "lesson of the heart," or a "trial of the affection," and who suffers the most sensitive and unheard of agonies. These works are usually in demand among young ladies with pale blue eyes and blonde curls—are bespoken some weeks ahead—and generally go the rounds of a family of several sisters, before they return to the library. When they are gathered in, they always bear feeble evidences of the mild delight experienced in their perusal, by light pencil marks under sentences like the following: "Mary did not answer but pressed her hand convulsively to her heart," or "the Rev. Mr. Lecturn turned away with a look of grave tenderness," or "the spirit strove with the flesh," and faint brackets enclosing whole paragraphs of attenuated sentiment and moral pathos. Although this bland criticism prevails in this style of literature and among these people, it would seem as if very few readers, even of the better class, could refrain from improving this opportunity to go to posterity side by side with their favorite authors. Perhaps there is something seductive in the attitude of the commentator, or the functions of the critic are more universal than we imagine. Lately, in looking over a copy of Montaigne, I found that some ingenious rebel sympathizer had complacently underscored, with comments, certain passages, which, to him seemed to justify his course. But the sympathizer was followed, on the same page and in the opposite margin, by a fierce loyal pencil, unsparing in epithet, and bitterly sarcastic on the first commentator. Nevertheless, I could not help smiling to think how the old egotistical Michael would have been astonished to have found himself, after three centuries of rest, occupying his old position in a civil war, as wordy at least as any that ever disturbed his conservatism in the flesh. For my own part, whenever I come upon anything of this kind that does not please me, I do not seek to answer or refute, but providing myself with a piece of India-rubber I calmly rub out the offensive commentary, and thus consign the critic to oblivion. If all ridiculous and unnecessary criticism could be as easily treated, how quickly might the world be freed from feeble and enfeebling controversies.

The habits and manners of certain visitors have fallen more or less under my observations. While I look with distrust on that man, who, having a home, prefers deliberately to sit down to the perusal of novel or romance in a public library,

I am by no means of the opinion that he should be tortured,
by unnecessary violence and interruption, to forego his right.
But I do not think that the opinion which some visitors entertain—that the appropriate mien for the occasion is a deportment, in which the solemnity of the church-goer and the pity-
ing concern of the hospital-visitor are blended—can be said to
be properly based. It will be noticed that excessively careful
people, in their anxiety to preserve silence, invariably drop a
large quarto on the floor, and precipitate a whole shelf in ruins
in their frantic efforts to save it. These people usually involve
themselves in difficulties with the ladder, ascending that instrument at perilous angles, which bring them presently to
grief and lamentation. There is the man who repeats the titles
of books audibly, as he walks beside the shelves; the three
young ladies who giggle quite as audibly, and who evidently
have intentions ulterior to the mere choice of reading matter;
the two or three young men, observant of the preceding party
yet apparently engaged in studious employment; the man
who is hunting authorities, and who is sternly scornful of
everybody else and their business; the confidential young
lady who requests the librarian to recommend some nice
book; the pale theologian, personally aggrieved that Bishop
Simpkins' admirable pamphlet on Transubstantiation is not
found in the catalogue, and the stern moralist who objects
that several infidel works *are* to be found therein; the envious
man, who longs for the book another has just taken out, and
the generous man, who drops in to find himself charged for an
interminable array of volumes, taken out by his friends, and
himself estopped of his privileges; these are among the individual peculiarities of the library. Add to this the feeling,
shared, I think, by all human kind, that the absence of any
book we particularly want is a kind of personal affront to ourselves—that librarian and directors are in some way privy to
the fact and responsible for it—and you have the general
psychological aspect of this, and, indeed, all circulating libraries. In regard to the Reading Room, I regret to say that

its moral tone is not quite up to that of the adjacent apartments. A thin vein of selfishness is apt to pervade it. The man who reads two sides of the *Bulletin* at once, and holds the supplement in his hand, may be fairly supposed to be capable of any enormity. But what shall be said of him, who, lying in wait on the arrival of the steamer, secures *Punch* and the *Saturday Review*, by sitting on them while he peruses the *Illustrated News*. On the other hand, I fancy it would require a man of some nerve to give himself completely up to the calm enjoyment of a magazine or newspaper, with the shadow of some hungry member impending over his page.

When the business of the day is over and the endless procession of changing faces is past; when the janitor turns the key, and the green baize door swings on its hinges for the last time, I can fancy that the sealed lips of the silent intelligences ranged around the wall, are suddenly opened, and that they babble pleasantly together in the style and fashion of their authors; that perhaps the quaint critics and essayists of the past century, from the dignity of a shelf to themselves, pronounce upon the new comers of the present day; that with ponderous sentences Dr. Johnson silences all pretensions, and occasionally even brow-beats the criticism of his fellow essayists, while Mr. Joseph Addison, in finely periwigged phrases, moralizes upon the vanity and illusion of authorship.

BRET.

CALIFORNIAN, *September 30, 1865.*

CHAPTER VII

Ana

THE tender calm and kindliness of the moonlit evenings during the past week, have offered such a contrast to the usual austerities of our summer nights, that the popular voice never wearies of hymning their praises. Yet it is a proof of the rarity of really pleasant weather in this climate, rather than of any logical acumen or scientific knowledge on the part of San Franciscans, that they invariably look with suspicion upon this atmospheric blandness, and, with a vague idea of the laws of compensation, call it "earthquake weather." The terrible suggestiveness of this epithet does not, however, interfere with the enjoyment of these lovely days and celestial nights. The roads leading toward Seal Rock, the Ocean House, and San Bruno have been nightly crowded with vehicles; the thoroughfares, especially the Portrero Bridge, have been filled with promenaders. I should have, perhaps, given the preference to the bridge as the most democratic and economical medium of enjoyment but for a recent experience. One night while strolling over it, felicitating myself upon the appearance of the city as it lay bathed in mysterious moonlight—its harsh, unfinished, and uncouth outlines subdued and mellowed; upon the glancing waters of the bay, flashing with bright lights here and there against the piles or about the hull of some shadowy outlying bark; upon the passing promenaders linked together in mystic couples, suddenly and without a note of preparation, but with evident deliberation and malice aforethought, one of a file of young ladies and gentlemen directly before me saw fit to lift her voice in song. We have the authority of Shakespeare certainly, that

> ———"soft stillness and the night
> Becomes the touches of sweet harmony,"

but it is somewhat questionable if "You will not forget me, mother," even when aided by a strong masculine chorus, is appropriate or soothing to the spirits at such a moment. At all events, possibly owing to some harmonious deficiency in my breast, some strategic and treasonable quality which forbade my being moved "by concord of sweet sounds," the effect of this *obligato* was terribly disenchanting. The hard outline of the hills seemed to come back; a key-note of the breezy shrillness of our summer afternoons was struck in that strong-minded female's voice, and I touched the earth again. Surely, if the privileges of a public performer were taken by her, the usual privileges of an audience in expressing approval or disapproval belonged to me.

A few nights after this experience I was induced to try the Cliff House road, in a buggy, with a companion. The evening was singularly beautiful and propitious. As we bowled along over the crumbling gravel, the toll-keeper, who started out of the magical moonlight and mysterious stillness, might have given us tickets to some celestial city, beyond the dread valley of the shadow of death, whose gleaming tombs we rattled so irreverently by, and whose cross, afar on a lonely hill, glittered and glanced beside us. The moon, riding high, touched the rough rocks as tenderly as though they were the crags of Latmos, forgetful that our western shepherds sleep with one eye open, and always make the first advances. The light on the Farrallones flashed out and was lost ere we could fix it. Sometimes, on entering a little valley, we would come upon a thin strata or current of warm air, as though a summer noon had got belated in the hills and lost its way in traveling westward. But the influence of the locality soon became fatally

apparent. Our horse, whom my companion addressed as
"Billy," but who, from a certain peculiarity of gait, I men-
tally christened "The Macadamizer," was what is called "a
fast horse." To him the moonlight and beatitudes of scenery
only suggested action. In an unlucky moment a rash individual attempted to pass us. "The Macadamizer" gave one
wild dash, afforded us a twinkling glimpse of all his four hoofs
at once and darted forward at headlong speed. We shot far
ahead of the infelix stranger; but this triumph seemed only to
incite "Macadamizer" to more frantic efforts. Far ahead he
sniffed a rival. The loose gravel and flinty rock flew to pieces
beneath his hammering hoofs. The buggy no longer rolled
along, but lifted itself in convulsive leaps as though it were
possessed of a desire to mount the back of our ambitious
steed. As I turned to my companion and mildly remonstrated
against the inappropriate and unharmonious character of
these proceedings, I was horror-struck at his apparent trans-
formation. By nature and education calm-eyed, even-voiced,
quiet and refined—delicately organized and free from demon-
strative action—this man was totally demoralized by the
wild "Macadamizer!" His hat was pushed back from his
thoughtful brow; his teeth were set, his hands grasped the
reins firmly—there was no mistaking it—a secret and guilty
sympathy existed between him and the relentless "Macadamizer." Under the deceitful and ostentatious show of rein-
ing in this ambitious animal, he was actually urging him to
greater effort. In vain I pointed to the stars in their regular
and carefully graduated orbits. Outwardly assenting to the
truth of my suggestions, calmly assuring me of his perfect
sympathy, he succeeded so completely in controlling "Macadamizer," that, in a few seconds, we not only overtook and
passed that particular stranger, but indeed all others on the
road. It is but just to him to state that, this position having
been attained, he fully and sincerely joined me in deploring
the process, with an eloquence perhaps a little heightened by
the success of the result. But alas! for our æsthetic enjoy-

ment. The *genus loci* had asserted itself. We were no longer pilgrims to the celestial city; no longer disciples of Thoreau in rapt sympathy with nature, but the proprietors of a fast horse, with Foster and whisky in the perspective.

———

PROSCRASTINATION is not the only form in which Time may be abstracted. There exist individuals who, under less vague and general titles, indulge in peculation of this synonym for money. The Time-thief differs from the usual highwayman; the latter limits his despoilations usually to strangers—the former compels his most intimate friend to stand and deliver. No place can be guarded against his entrance; the counting-room, the private office, the editorial sanctum, is opened by the skeleton key of courtesy, which fits all locks and opens all doors. Once in, the Time-thief proceeds to prosecute his unhallowed calling. You are writing an important business letter; you are engaged on an editorial, or you are drawing a brief. The Time-thief begins by an artful display of frankness. He sees you are busy, he will not detain you a moment—he himself is busy, etc., etc. Beguiled by his remark, you drop your pen, and utter some confused and meaningless apology, with a vacant smile. The Time-thief begins haply with an allusion to your letter, your editorial, or your brief. For a few moments he is bearable, sometimes interesting. But, speedily dropping your business, he suddenly changes to his own. Common courtesy, of course, forbids a too rapid change on your part. So you listen: at first resignedly, then with an unmistakable distraction of the eye, which will, after a formal circuit of the room, wander back to your manuscript. You make a feeble show of taking up your pen and punctuating your composition, or of crossing a *t*, or retouching the tail of a *y*. At intervals, you utter an indefinite response, which you mildly hope may be taken for affirmation or negation, as the case may be. These signs affect the Time-thief no more than the struggles of the victim affect the garroter. But he is not altogether unmindful of them; no one knows better than he how much the victim can bear. When a sternness settles around your mouth, and a preliminary cough rises to your lips, he leaves his seat as if to retire apologetically with his booty. Rash is the victim who at this moment is betrayed into softness—the movement was but a *ruse*; he has enlisted your attention, which was all he wanted, and he succeeds in appropriating five minutes more to his ill gotten gains.

———

It may be questioned whether Church Fairs or Festivals, as a means of collecting charity or contributions, are not in their decade. The old-fashioned Pious Bazaars and Serious Thread and Needle Shops have given way to Festivals and Charades, and it has been found necessary to approximate more closely to worldly entertainments for worldly patronage. Yet there was and still is a certain pleasure in viewing the pretty saints, who, in most cases, keep shop under pleasing and appropriate *aliases*. Who has not felt a thrill at being importuned by Hope to buy a ticket in a raffle; or blushed when Faith called upon him to exercise her peculiar talent, and blindly and fondly put his hand into a green bag, under the pleasing delusion of drawing out something worth having. Who does not recall the pleasing expectation with which he received the news that a letter was lying for him in the post-office, which missive, with his name prominently misspelled, he found to be filled with bland generalities. Whither have ye fled, "O blue-eyed banditti," who were wont to dart out of evergreen ambush upon the spruce young traveller and despoil him of his coin? Where are the refreshments which seemed like "locusts and wild honey" to the Sunday-school boy, and the marble "sody" fountain, which, to him, appeared even as the gushing rock, struck by the Mosaic hand?

———

To a reflective mind, I dare say that the street cars afford excellent opportunities of studying humanity in sincerer forms, and at more advantageous focal distances than people suppose. The short interval of time in which strangers are thrown together leaves them no opportunity for deception. Snobs of either sex are apt to display their foibles even in the passage of a block. I am reminded of an incident which occurred in my experience, and which, at the time, I put into the pleasing and ever popular form, of a fable. I venture, in absence of more serious matter, to repeat it here.

THE FABLE OF BEAUTY, THE BEAST, AND THE PERFECT GENT— FOR GOOD LITTLE GIRLS AND BOYS

BEAUTY was one day shopping on Montgomery street, and, getting quite weary, she thought she would ride. So she stopped a car. But when poor Beauty came to the door, and looked in, she saw it was full. Then a Beast, who was sitting by the door grumbled, "All full inside," and looked at Beauty as though he would eat her up. But a Perfect Gent got up from his seat and said: "Take my seat, dear Beauty, and I will stand up." Then Beauty smiled at the Perfect Gent; and the other Gents who were not Perfect said to each other: "Let us bust the crust of this Perfect Gent and black his eye." But while they were whispering among themselves, an Ugly Old Woman stopped the car and squeaked out: "Is there any room?" Then the Perfect Gent said, "All full inside;" but, to everybody's astonishment, the Beast got out and said to the Ugly Old Woman: "Take my seat." But the Perfect Gent jumped and took the Beast's seat, and pulled the bell so that the driver drove on, leaving the Beast and the Ugly Old Woman in the middle of the street. This made the passengers and the the Perfect Gent laugh very much, for it was a Joke.

Moral.—This fable teaches us that we should endeavor to be a Beauty and a Perfect Gent, rather than a Beast or an Ugly Old Woman. Also, that whatever wrong a Beast may attempt, he will sooner or later be punished at the hands of a Perfect Gent. O, what a nice thing it is to be a Perfect Gent!

BRET.

CALIFORNIAN, *November* 4, 1865.

THE CLIFF HOUSE OF THE SIXTIES

CHAPTER VIII

A Blow on the Cliff

W HEN the fierce southwester of the past week was at its height, and the Oakland ferry-boat failed to make a landing at its accustomed wharf; when tall ships dragged their anchors, and umbrellas flew from the excited grasp of pedestrians; when signboards were loosed, tin roofs stripped off, and the "storm-wind Euroclydon" swept resistlessly through the deserted streets of San Francisco, two travellers in a buggy might have been seen breasting the blast on the desolate sandhills toward the ocean beach. But as at this point all resemblance to the opening chapters of a once popular novel ceased, I may as well admit that the two mysterious travellers were the present writer, and a companion, on their way to the Cliff House. The style of conveyance—whoever heard of a hero in a buggy?—the style of garment—India-rubber overcoats—were alone sufficient to unfit them for that romantic narrative which aims rather at the picturesque than the comfortable.

As we crept along, at times making scarcely any headway against the gale, which tore furiously across the road, charged with spray, that left upon our lips an ominous foretaste of the ocean, miles away, we noticed that the roar of the surf, at first quite perceptible, seemed to decrease as we approached the shore. The rain, mixed with flying particles of sand from the adjacent hills, stung our faces like the Lilliputian arrows discharged at Gulliver, and our "water-proofs"—alas! for the ingenuity of man—succumbed at last to the incessant beating of the storm. We finally sat in a douche bath, while from every angle of our garments the water poured in gentle rivulets, or from our hats dropped in a continuous "waterfall" behind. Our horse, the dauntless "Macadamizer"— albeit he had his own suspicions of the sanity of the two occupants of the buggy—butted away the storm from his broad shoulders, and, at last, "in the very tempest and whirlwind" of this elemental passion, we stood upon the balcony of the Cliff House.

Far as the eye could reach, or where the southerly trend of the beach mingled with the storm, and sky and shore line were blotted out by the driving scud, the whole vast expanse seemed to undulate with yawning caverns and toppling cliffs of water. Although the "yeasty surges" swept far up the beach, there was but little foam to seaward; the level gale sheared their white plumes almost as quickly as they heaved into sight, and drove them inland like the scattered down from some wild sea bird. The sand was covered with clinging patches of viscid spume thrown from the racing waves, as the foam is cast from the tossing bit of a thoroughbred. The lesser rocks, where the sea-lions were wont to bask in the sunlight, were scarcely ever free from the surging of tumultuous seas that boiled, hissed and seethed around them. At times a wave, larger than its fellows, charging upon the single peak known as "Seal Rock," and breaking half-way up its summit, would fling half its volume in snowy foam twenty feet above the crest, to fall and fill with a leaping torrent each ravine in the rocky flanks of the lonely peak. Far out to sea, wave after wave heaved their huge leaden sides like the dull scales of some undulating monster. Nearer in shore the billows were cleanly cut, but the fierce breeze dulled their edges, and they broke unevenly upon the sand.

The view was unsurpassed in grandeur. Whether from the windows of the parlor of the Cliff House, where but a single piece of plate-glass seemed to separate the comforts and refinements of civilization and peace from the rude jarring of elemental discord, and Nature in her rudest aspect, beyond. Whether from the cliff above, where we leaned against the wind, and looked down upon the gathering surf beneath our feet and the rollers hastening with impatient strides toward the Golden Gate, or whether from the beach itself, where huge trunks of spars were rolled and tossed like straws upon the sand, and where the waves raced like ravenous wolves, and it was perilous to venture. It was with a feeling of regret that we at last turned our faces—our cheeks buffeted by the elements into a healthy glow—once more toward the city, and exchanged the rough but hearty welcome of sea and shore for the blazing "sea-coal" and close windows of the town. BRET.

CALIFORNIAN, *November* 25, 1868.

CHAPTER IX

_____

The Fourth in the Suburbs

_____

BY THE AUTHOR OF "MY SUBURBAN RESIDENCE"

_____

I N INDEPENDENCE of all civic celebration and display, I have been spending the Fourth of July at my suburban residence. Let not the incautious reader suppose that my pleasures were purely bucolic or rural. I have not been unfamiliar with those ingenious contrivances which my youngest boy, in the imperfect orthœpy of youth, denominates as "fire-wax." Even as I write, a subtle, sulphurous flavor pervades the house; the garden walks are strewn with fragmentary and exploded crackers, whose red outer wrappers rustle in the breeze, as though they were the autumnal leaves of that Tree of Liberty which flourishes so pre-eminently at this season. The fences are blackened, remarkable blisters appear upon the white paint of the verandah, and the hand that records these experiences is grimy and black with powder.

The celebration of the day was opened with cheerful energy by a neighbor with a four-pounder. Apparently under the impression that his remoteness from the city limits justified him in an extra vigor of expression, he for a long time held a terrible pre-eminence in the neighborhood, dominating over all other sounds to that extent that the Chinese crackers of my children, albeit they were extra size, sank into puerile insignificance. He kept up this system of brain-shattering explosions, until I hit upon the expedient of upsetting at regular intervals a pile of clap-boards which stood conveniently in my back-yard, and which I am gratified to state produced a concussion, not only equal in intensity, but far superior in the matter of duration. This, or want of powder, silenced him eventually. My Newfoundland dog rendered me valuable assistance during the controversy by barking furiously, and charging the enemy's cannon violently, after each discharge.

In fact I had matured a plan of celebration of my own, with which this self asserting character of my neighbor's somewhat interfered. My eldest boy had been presented with a model of a Monitor, which had a practicable turret that moved by machinery, and I wished to turn the occasion to account. I accordingly constructed on the banks of a little pond in the rear of my lot, a small fortress, which I mounted with miniature practicable cannon, and garrisoned with a company of stolid and inflexible wooden soldiers, borrowed for the occasion from the nursery. A little distance from this frowning fortress I laid a mine, with a slow match. A few feet from the fort floated a model ship of war with a fine broadside (also practicable) of four guns. The fort bore a rebel flag, the ship-of-war carried the stars and stripes. When I state that I christened the fort, Fort Fisher, the reader will understand how my object was to combine instruction and patriotism, and to endeavor to exhibit to my children in mimic detail the events of that memorable engagement. The Monitor, which also mounted a small cannon in its turret, it is needless to say was kept in reserve until the proper moment.

With the exception of some slight incongruities, the effect of these details when completed was very fine. The fact that the rebel garrison was composed of giants—who might have been, in comparison with the size of the Union ship, roughly estimated at fifteen feet high—lent an additional moral effect to the victory which was to be achieved over them. At exactly twelve the ship of war was placed into position, with her guns covering the fort, and the slow matches lighted. An interval of breathless suspense followed. The audience, consisting of my two children, and a select deputation of young people from the neighboring houses, fairly trembled with excitement.

Bang!—the first gun from the ship. A cheer from the juveniles. No visible effect on the fort, but a decided splash in the water on the opposite side of the ship. On examination one gun was missing from her deck. General depression—with the exception of my youngest, who then and thereafter wildly cheered everything in a most extravagant manner.

The second gun was very appropriately fired from the fort. But, while it resembled the first in its harmlessness toward the object against which it was directed, it was attended by disastrous consequences within. The whole garrison instantly fell stiffly and immovably on their faces, with the exception of the rebel commander, who, being placed at a greater prominence on the parapet, calmly dropped over the rail, and remained standing on his head, with his inflexible feet in the air, coolly surveying the enemy during the rest of the engagement. The quiet unconcern he exhibited might have been the effect of discipline, or the conscious security of his position, for the next movement of the ship was to yaw and discharge with extreme rapidity the rest of her broadside into my party, who retired with some precipitation.

On returning to the scene of conflict, it was discovered that one of the rebel sentries had deliberately rolled down the bank into the water and was just then floating in a peculiarly imbecile and stiff-legged manner in the pond. A disagreeable smell of burning paint which was occasionally wafted from the fort, was found to proceed from another sentry who had been ignited by some burning wadding and was slowly being consumed from his legs upward, without any visible alteration in his military bearing or movement of his inflexible features. It was evident that the critical moment had come—the hour for decisive action had arrived. The rebel fort was already in a defenceless condition, but for the matter of that the Union war vessel was also in distress, with her shrouds on fire. I rapidly wound up the Monitor, set a slow match to her two redoubtable cannon, and amid the intensest excitement shoved her off. She proceeded toward Fort Fisher finely—although perhaps her turret revolved a little too rapidly to be consistent with the best facilities for aiming—until she arrived directly opposite, and then without the slightest apparent reason changed her course and threw herself with a fearful clicking of wheels full against the hapless Union vessel. Totally disregarding her duty to save the ship 'at all hazards, she deliberately bore her unfortunate ally to the opposite bank and discharged with frightful rapidity her two cannon, raking the deck of the defenceless vessel and blowing the remaining guns overboard. A thrill of horror ran through the spectators. But at this moment the sagacity of my noble Newfoundland dog who had been barking furiously at the whole proceeding, changed the aspect of affairs. Disregarding the fire of Fort Fisher, he sprang into the pond, sunk the Union vessel with one stroke of his paw, seized the Monitor whose turret still revolved frantically, and brought the vessel dripping to my feet. As a matter of course the mine, till then forgotten, took that opportunity to explode directly under one of the interested spectators.

The infelicities of the morning were repeated in the evening celebration. The exhibition of fire-works was remarkable, and some novel effects were introduced, but, on the whole, it could hardly be called successful. A thick fog enveloped the house, the wind blew chilly from the west, and the moisture dripped incessantly from the foliage. Some of the rockets sulked; those that were successfully ignited were completely controlled by the wind and took one uniform direction and angle in their flight. After I had despatched half a dozen, I received a courteous, but firm remonstrance from one of my neighbors, who informed me that, as their ultimate destination appeared to be his attic windows, he would like some explanation. His statement seemed credible from the fact that the rockets were lost in the fog almost as quickly as they rose. I sent by way of reply another, which I have since learned overtook the messenger, and fixed itself on the verandah, where, for some time, it played like a fiery hose over his garden bed. The Catherine wheels, after one or two revolutions, remained fixed, and derisively hissed at the spectators. A star mine, which had persistently refused to ignite, after having been returned to the parlor, suddenly sprang into fearful activity, sent up a brilliant and variously-tinted shower of sparks into the chandelier, and finally had to be quenched ignominiously by the garden hose. Only the Bengola Lights acted consistently. *They* burned steadily, with a baleful and peculiarly wicked glare, lighting up the disastrous scene, apparently enjoying the discomfiture of my audience, and investing them with a ghastly solemnity. They burned long after the entertainment was concluded, and one of them, fixed upon the fence, still lends its ominous light as I write these experiences.

CALIFORNIAN, *July* 7, 1866.

CHAPTER X

𝔐e

BY SIR ED—D L—TT—N B—LW—R

[1][Anxious to keep up the literary standard of The Californian, its proprietors have, at an enormous expense, recently engaged the principal novelists of Europe and America to contribute to its columns. In view of the objections sometimes offered to "Only a Clod" and other continued tales, arrangements have been made with the different authors to condense their stories into a space that shall not exceed two columns of our paper. By this means The Californian will be enabled to offer its readers a three-volume novel in a single issue, or so to speak, a seventy-five cent book for ten cents. By the last steamer, we have received our third installment, from the pen of an elegant and philosophical writer, which we give below:]

BOOK I

THE PROMPTINGS OF THE IDEAL

I T WAS noon. Sir Edward had stepped from his brougham and was proceeding on foot down the Strand. He was dressed with his usual faultless taste, but in alighting from his vehicle his foot slipped, and a small round disk of conglomerated soil, which instantly appeared on his high arched instep, marred the harmonious glitter of his boots. Sir Edward was fastidious. Casting his eyes around, at a little distance he perceived the stand of a youthful bootblack. Thither he sauntered, and carelessly placing

---

[1]I am reprinting this story with the original title and the introduction. In the later versions the title was changed and the introduction dropped.—Editor.

his foot on the low stool, he awaited the application of the polisher's Art. "'Tis true," said Sir Edward to himself, yet half aloud, "the contact of the Foul and the Disgusting mars the general effect of the Shiny and the Beautiful—and, yet, why am I here? I repeat it, calmly and deliberately—why am I here? Ha! Boy!"

The Boy looked up—his dark Italian eyes glanced intelligently at the Philosopher, and, as with one hand he tossed back his glossy curls from his marble brow, and with the other he spread the equally glossy Day & Martin over the Baronet's boot, he answered in deep rich tones: "The Ideal is subjective to the Real. The exercise of apperception gives a distinctiveness to idiocracy, which is, however, subject to the limits of ME. You are an admirer of the Beautiful, sir. You wish your boots blacked. The Beautiful is attainable by means of the Coin."

"Ah," said Sir Edward thoughtfully, gazing upon the almost supernal beauty of the Child before him; "you speak well. You have read *Kant*."

The Boy blushed deeply. He drew a copy of *Kant* from his blouse, but in his confusion several other volumes dropped from his bosom on the ground. The Baronet picked them up.

"Ah!" said the Philosopher, "what's this? *Cicero's De Senectute*, at your age, too? *Martial's Epigrams, Cæsar's Commentaries*. What! a classical scholar?"

"E pluribus Unum. Nux vomica. Nil desperandum. Nihil fit!" said the Boy, enthusiastically. The Philosopher gazed at the Child. A strange presence seemed to transfuse and possess him. Over the brow of the Boy glittered the pale nimbus of the Student.

"Ah, and Schiller's *Robbers*, too?" queried the Philosopher.

"Das ist ausgespielt," said the Boy modestly.

"Then you have read my translation of *Schiller's Ballads*?" continued the Baronet, with some show of interest.

"I have, and infinitely prefer them to the original," said the Boy, with intellectual warmth. "You have shown how in

Actual life we strive for a Goal we cannot reach; how in the Ideal the Goal is attainable, and there effort is victory. You have given us the Antithesis which is a key to the Remainder, and constantly balances before us the conditions of the Actual and the privileges of the Ideal."

"My very words," said the Baronet; "wonderful, wonderful," and he gazed fondly at the Italian boy, who again resumed his menial employment. Alas! the wings of the Ideal were folded. The Student had been absorbed in the Boy.

But Sir Edward's boots were blacked, and he turned to depart. Placing his hand upon the clustering tendrils that surrounded the classic nob of the infant Italian, he said softly, like a strain of distant music:

"Boy, you have done well. Love the Good. Protect the Innocent. Provide for the Indigent. Respect the Philosopher." . . . . "Stay! Can you tell me what *is* The True, The Beautiful, The Innocent, The Virtuous?"

"They are things that commence with a capital letter," said the Boy, promptly.

"Enough! Respect everything that commences with a capital letter! Respect ME!" and dropping a half-penny in the hand of the Boy, he departed.

The Boy gazed fixedly at the coin. A frightful and instantaneous change overspread his features. His noble brow was corrugated with baser lines of calculation. His black eye, serpent-like, glittered with suppressed passion. Dropping upon his hands and feet, he crawled to the curbstone and hissed after the retreating form of the Baronet, the single word:

"Bilk!" ——

BOOK II
IN THE WORLD

"Eleven years ago," said Sir Edward to himself, as his brougham slowly rolled him toward the Committee Room; "just eleven years ago my natural son disappeared mysteri-

ously. I have no doubt in the world but that this little bootblack is he. His mother died in Italy. He resembles his mother
very much. Perhaps I ought to provide for him. Shall I disclose myself? No! no! Better he should taste the sweets of
Labor. Penury ennobles the mind and kindles the Love of the
Beautiful. I will act to him, not like a Father, not like a
Guardian, not like a Friend—but like a Philosopher!"

With these words, Sir Edward entered the Committee
Room. His Secretary approached him. "Sir Edward, there
are fears of a division in the House, and the Prime Minister
has sent for you."

"I will be there," said Sir Edward, as he placed his hand on
his chest and uttered a hollow cough!

No one who heard the Baronet that night, in his sarcastic
and withering speech on the Drainage and Sewerage Bill,
would have recognized the Lover of the Ideal and the Philosopher of the Beautiful. No one who listened to his eloquence
would have dreamed of the Spartan resolution this iron man
had taken in regard to the Lost Boy—his own beloved Lionel.
None!

"A fine speech from Sir Edward, to-night," said Lord Bil-
lingsgate, as, arm-and-arm with the Premier, he entered his
carriage.

"Yes! but how dreadfully he coughs!"

"Exactly. Dr. Bolus says his lungs are entirely gone; he
breathes entirely by an effort of will, and altogether independent of pulmonary assistance."

"How strange!" and the carriage rolled away.

BOOK III

THE DWELLER OF THE THRESHOLD

"Adon Ai, appear! appear!"

And as the Seer spoke, the awful Presence glided out of
Nothingness, and sat, sphinxlike, at the feet of the Alchemist.

"I am come!" said the Thing.

"You should say, 'I have come'—it's better grammar," said the Boy-Neophyte, thoughtfully accenting the substituted expression.

"Hush, rash Boy," said the Seer sternly. "Would you oppose your feeble knowledge to the infinite intelligence of the Unmistakable. A word, and you are lost forever."

The Boy breathed a silent prayer, and handing a sealed packet to the Seer, begged him to hand it to his father in case of his premature decease.

"You have sent for me," hissed the Presence. "Behold me, Apokatharticon—the Unpronounceable. In me all things exist that are not already co-existent. I am the Unattainable, the Intangible, the Cause and the Effect. In me observe the Brahma of Mr. Emerson; not only Brahma himself, but also the sacred musical composition rehearsed by the faithful Hindoo. I am the real Gyges. None others are genuine."

And the veiled Son of the Starbeam laid himself loosely about the room, and permeated Space generally.

"Unfathomable Mystery," said the Rosicrucian in a low, sweet voice. Brave Child with the Vitreous Optic! Thou who pervadest all things and rubbest against us without abrasion of the cuticle. I command thee, speak!"

And the misty, intangible, indefinite Presence spoke.

————

BOOK IV

MYSELF

After the events related in the last chapter, the reader will perceive that nothing was easier than to reconcile Sir Edward to his son Lionel, nor to resuscitate the beautiful Italian girl, who, it appears, was not dead, and to cause Sir Edward to marry his first and boyish love whom he had deserted. They were married in St. George's Hanover Square. As the bridal party stood before the altar, Sir Edward, with a sweet, sad smile, said, in quite his old manner:

"The Sublime and Beautiful are the Real; the only Ideal is the Ridiculous and Homely. Let us always remember this. Let us through life endeavor to personify the virtues, and always begin 'em with a capital letter. Let us, whenever we can find an opportunity, deliver our sentiments in the form of round hand copies. Respect the Aged. Eschew Vulgarity. Admire Ourselves. Regard the Novelist."

CALIFORNIAN, *July* 15. 1865.

CHAPTER XI

A Few Operatic Criticisms

I WOULD state at the beginning of this article that I am not an opera critic, and do not wish to be confounded with any of those amiable gentlemen who write the regular notices, whose facile handling of musical terms always impresses me, and who, with their other varied talents seem to be gifted with a prescience which not unfrequently enables them to pen a fair description of a performance before it has taken place. But I deem it only just to these gentlemen to say that their criticisms partake of all the vagueness and obscurity of the prophetic statement, are susceptible of a variety of meanings, and convey a certain impressiveness which a careful analysis fails to substantiate.

My object being to ask rather than give information, to make suggestions rather than statements, I find myself at this point somewhat embarrassed by my style, which has in the first paragraph unwittingly assumed something of the didactic and critical quality I have deprecated. Writing purely from a sense of ignorance I find myself unconsciously in that oracular attitude which any excess of this quality is apt to produce. To come to the point from which I have been straying, I should like to propound a few questions.

Why are baritones—with the exception of "Don Giovanni," "Plunkett" and a few others—always either unsuccessful in love or inimical to its expression? Why are they invariably jilted lovers, cruel parents or hated elder brothers?

Is there anything in their quality of voice which precludes a perfect illustration of reciprocal passion? Believing this arbitrary rule would fail in real life, it has occurred to me that it might be an interesting experiment for the tenor and baritone to sometimes change places. But then, it has also occurred to me that the tenor, owing to what I conceive to be his natural weakness, would fail completely; his vindictiveness would be apt to be feminine and hysterical, his malice would be inconceivably shrill, and would naturally take small methods of expression; instead of using the dagger he would probably pinch the soprano and call the baritone bad names. His passion is of a quality so evidently made to be appreciated—his existence is so peculiarly dependent upon the soprano who is the female of his species, that I shudder to think of his conduct under any of those conditions which bring out the baritone so splendidly. As the tenor voice expresses the highest musical standard of masculine perfection, I have sometimes wondered if the weaknesses I have described were not incidental to other qualities of perfection. But I fear that I am wandering from the subject at this point, and pass on to the next question.

Why are the chorus always so unanimous in their expressions of sympathy? Would not some slight diversity of opinion, or a little independence of character on the part of one or two, be an agreeable relief, besides throwing a little more sincerity into their condolence or congratulations? But I have noticed that in spite of this apparent sympathy for the principal actor, they invariably ignore each other's acquaintance on the stage, and stand apart even while uttering a sentiment in which they all concur. Their relations are so evidently to the baritone or tenor, and so little to each other, that if I were a composer I should consider it my duty to write an opera that should be all chorus, just to throw these gentlemen back upon themselves and develop their individuality. They are so utterly dependent upon the principal characters for their ideas, and sometimes even for their language, that the spectacle often becomes humiliating to the sensitive man, and I can readily imagine that a continued habit of chorus singing is dreadfully shattering to character. I am not prepared to say that their peculiarities are unreal, or their conduct unnatural. On the contrary, I have met in this real world one or two distinguished men who seem to have been attended through life by just such sympathizing choruses. Like these operatic brethren, this worldly chorus have neither reciprocity nor individuality; they are not warmed by the sentiments they echo, and if the actor to whom they are related is removed they have nothing to do but transfer their relations to some other. Born to the chorus they never rise in their profession—but feeling that I am guilty of a certain complicity with T. S. Arthur and Miss Braddon in the construction of this moral, I leave the sentence unfinished.

Why does the vernacular in English Opera—particularly in recitative—always affect us unpleasantly, irrespective of its musical infelicity? Perhaps we instinctively acknowledge a certain discord between our real sentiments and expression' and the delightful shams and tinselled rhetoric set up before us. I have noticed that as long as the language of the libretto is confined to the French and Italian idioms, we seldom trouble ourselves about its morality or truthfulness to Nature, and rather believe that the responsibility in some way devolves on those nations in whose language the opera is written. The scrofulous sentiment of Camille, so unbearable in the dialogue of the English play, is altogether changed in the delicious music and "soft bastard Latin" of Traviata. For these reasons I am inclined to believe that those barbarians who decry Italian opera because they cannot understand the language, are not as honest as they would have us think. What business have they to want to understand it? Why should they drag the prosaic utterances of their every day life into the region of romance and poetry?

But the philosopher who analyses his pleasures loses half

his enjoyment, and the gods destroy those who scrutinize their gifts. Wherefore, O reader, let you and I proceed quietly to the temple of enchantment, in which a questioning word or doubt dissolves the charm. Let us look cheerfully upon this brilliant assembly, and the lovely creatures attired in that charming full dress in which, alas, so few of the real heroic duties of womanly life are performed. The curtain rises. Smile not, scoffer, because the silver moon, which ascends with such alarming rapidity over the Druid groves, is several times larger than the one with which thou art familiarly acquainted. Pretermit the jest which rises to thy lips at the imperial which the stoutest Druid, who is unfamiliar with early English history, sports upon his chin. Question not the theology of the Priestess, for the rippling curls of the lady before thee are false, the diamond that glitters on the bosom of yonder snob is paste. We are such stuff as operas are made of, and our little life is rounded by the fall of the green curtain.

BRET.

CALIFORNIAN, *May* 13, 1865.

CHAPTER XII

Audiences

I HAVE often found it a relief to transfer my attention from a dull play or a prosy lecture to the audience around me. I cannot say that the result of such observations has always been to impress me with a profound sense of their aggregate discernment or judgment. The conviction usually forced upon me, was, that audiences were at the best, mobs—differing from other mobs in good nature, and in the fact that they have been called together for pleasure instead of business, but, nevertheless, as utterly swayed by prejudice, as deaf to reason, as completely under the dominion of one or two leaders, and as lost to a sense of individual responsibility as any mob that was ever dispersed by grape-shot. I have seen audiences to whom the Riot Act might have properly been read. It is not necessary to get up an alarm of fire in the dress circle of the opera to prove this, and show how speedily an assemblage of dress-coats and opera hats will resolve itself into its original, selfish and unreasoning elements. The most trifling circumstances are sufficient to establish the fact. Yet, if I were to tell intelligent theatre-goers that their position in the parquette or the dress circle transformed them for the time being, from sensible and independent men into fools and cowards, they would consider themselves insulted. If I were to walk up to my friend Fitz Flunk as he has ceased applauding, and leans complacently against the wall, and inform him that he was not expressing his own sentiments but those of Bill Smith in the gallery, simply because Bill was possessed of a louder voice, heavier boots and greater self-assertion, he would look upon me as crazy. What would the

readers of this journal say if I were to bribe its musical critic
to allow me to displace his regular notice of the opera, wherein he speaks about the "commendation of an appreciative
audience" and "tremendous applause," with a notice like the
following:

"The Opera House on —— evening was the scene of a
most disgraceful exhibition during the performance of Verdi's
magnificent opera of *The Marrowbones and Cleavers*. At the
conclusion of the *romanza* in the second act, Signor Batti
Batti saw fit to favor the audience with a few notes not in the
composer's score, which a few ignorant persons in the pit
choose to encore. A slight token of dissent from one or two in
the dress circle increased this encore to a tumultuous enthusiasm, and Signor Batti Batti was obliged, though bursting
with laughter, to repeat the *romanza*, innovation and all. To
render the exhibition more disgraceful, we noticed that the
better portion of the audience laughed, and that the few who
were justly indignant were evidently restrained, by the fear
of making themselves prominent, from expressing their sentiments."

The universal criticism of a notice of that kind would be
that the writer was hypercritical, and had misunderstood the
"generosity" of a San Francisco audience. But what if this
generosity lead us to injustice? what if it can be proved that
it is owing to this "generosity," or tacit abnegation of the
tastes and privileges of the individual members of an audience
that the drama deteriorates, or that the standard of taste is
lowered, or that sensation plays take the place of Shakspeare?
What if I, who, as stated at the beginning of this article, prefer to turn from the spectacle of a stupid play to the more interesting occupation of watching the audience, by foregoing
my right to hiss or express disapprobation, become accessory
to the reproduction of this piece. Why do I wink at my friend
on the opposite side of the house, whom I know participates
in my sentiments, instead of openly expressing my feelings.
Why do I convey my adverse criticism to my neighbor in a

whisper. Surely there is no terrorism that should prevent a frank avowal. The short-haired "rough" in the pit, expresses his delight boisterously, and would, I have no doubt, express his dissatisfaction, should he have occasion so to do, as strongly. Am I to blame the manager or the critic if he fail to appreciate my reserve, and accept the rough's criticism?

It is not only in regard to the intrinsic merits or demerits of a performance that audiences show themselves to be governed by this mob influence. It is felt in the graver question of morals. When some impure god in the gallery sees fit to put an equivocal construction on the words of a pretty actress, and so applauds from the depths of his filthy soul, not only do the more decent—by refraining from outspoken indignation —accept the false construction, but too often encourage it by imbecile smiling. I have seen old Silenus under cover of this mob influence, and solely because he was in a theatre, chuckle audibly in his seat beside a young girl, at an expression which in his own house he would not dared to have noticed. I have seen young ladies, led on by the same unconscious influence, simpering at a dubious sentiment, in a manner that would leave the spectator to suppose they had handed in their modesty with their tickets at the door. In society the refuge from such attacks is insensibility and indifference; in a mixed audience there are always too many self-constituted interpreters. It is the misconstruction and unfair handling of this latest error, which gives to the Gradgrinds and Huntingdons a mischievous weapon in their attacks on the morality of the theatre.

So manifestly unfair is the usual *viva voce* manner of taking the "sense of the house," that most of the encores are usually given for the benefit of four or five ingenious and selfish individuals, whose strength of lungs and facilities for holding out beyond the usual limit of applause are always successful. The occasion may be singularly inopportune; the prima donna may be exhausted, the opera may be dragging already beyond the usual limit, but no matter, the leader turns over the leaves of his score, and orchestra and singer go back and begin again. I would here remark that these and other spontaneous outbursts are not always an evidence of musical conception. The genuine taste of these gushing enthusiasts who break in upon a *scena* or the *cadenza* of a prima donna, to exhibit their foolish appreciation, may be reasonably questioned.

It must be admitted, then, there is something to be said on the other side of the question. A really intelligent and appreciative audience are apt to appear cold and critical. The highest form of approval does not take upon itself vehement outward expression; the best acting, the purest music, the noblest sentiment, do not awaken extravagant and boisterous applause. The audiences who listened to the Keans might have seemed unsympathetic and cold to a casual spectator who had just left the minstrels, although the amount of enjoyment experienced by both audiences might have been equal. But there is something in this placid and correct satisfaction which is apt to chill the spectator—not to speak of the actors—if too long indulged, and the avidity with which a poor pun, or a grimace, or even the *contretemps* of some unfortunate supernumerary, is seized upon as the pretext for a thoughtless laugh, is an evidence of the weakness of even the best audiences. Some audiences require to be set into approbatory motion, as others require to be retarded in their applause. Who has not felt the awkwardness of finding himself a solitary applauder, and the delight at hearing, after a brief interval, a confirmatory echo from other parts of the house? We need not go to France to learn the importance of *claquers*. A friend, who had faced many critical audiences, once told me that he always found it necessary to throw out some pleasant trifle to the *oi polloi*, by way of "humanizing" and equalizing his listeners, as well as of warming himself by their contagious laughter. The first laugh—the first applause—the first cheer—is always the most difficult; that done, the rest is easy. Applause is not always spontaneous; a few quick perceptions seize the point, and there is what the reporters call "a sensation." Then come a few rattling shots, and finally—the volley.

All audiences are alike as all human nature is alike. They are more apt to act upon impulse than deliberation; they find it easier to be led than to lead; to fall in with the current than to oppose it. If this is true of the ordinary business of life it is equally true of the pleasures. Until men shall be thoughtful enough to make even their pleasure subservient to their moral and intellectual advancement, we must not look for decisive judgments from popular audiences.   BRET.

CALIFORNIAN, *August* 5, 1865

CHAPTER XIII

Under the Weather

A FIT of sickness is apt to enlarge a man's capacity for observation and impression. Even an ordinary cold will sometimes go far toward finishing his education. To poor people sickness is often a refining process; it tones down organizations where the animal predominates; reflection and reading is encouraged, and the patient is isolated from the temptations and distractions of cheap pleasure. I don't mean those common inflammatory disturbances which throw up temporary barricades in all the avenues of expression without affecting any constitutional reform, but a sickness that shall throw you over on your side like the strapped Cruiser, and indulge in cruel aggravations over your helpless form. A man under such circumstances will receive moral ethics with his calomel, and take in grains of wisdom with his quinine.

Some people take sickness as a personal affront. Physicians will tell you that it is difficult to make certain individuals believe that there is not a peculiarity about their symptoms which at once segregates them from the great mass of suffering humanity and renders their case particularly difficult to treat. There are others who go to the opposite extreme, who have all the symptoms which affect their friends, and who show their good faith and sincerity by swallowing their medicines. But I propose to give a few of the psychological phenomena, leaving out those dreadful symptoms which are thrown up in inverted pyramids in Ayer's, Brandeth's and Sands' advertisements, and which you meet in all the medical books:

To lie awake with a strong consciousness that you ought to be asleep. To be morbidly alive to distant footsteps, to the rumble of carriage wheels and the half-hummed chants of obscure night birds going home to roost. To hear the ticking of near clocks and the hour tolled from the Cathedral tower, taken up by smaller chimes, and closed, after a minute's lapse, when you are trying once more to shut the windows of your soul, by some laggard and reluctant clock in your neighborhood. To listen to all the fire alarms, and speculate upon the locality and the probability of the fire spreading. To settle in your mind the best place to tie your sheets and coverlid if obliged to make your escape by the window. To be immediately afterward precipitated into a doze, and dream that you have done so, but are embarrassed by the lightness of your apparel. To have a deep scorn for others who are asleep and to have a strong conviction that sleep is the natural refuge for stupidity. To hear people laugh in the street and to feel personally aggrieved at their levity. To have a strong disposition to sit up, and upon doing so to have an equal disposition to lie down again and try it all over. To notice the last stroke of the mason's trowel on the ceiling and have a strong inclination to match the wall paper more correctly. To have the shadowy bed curtains suggest outlines of concealed figures. To notice a crack in your dressing case that you never noticed before. To catch a sight of somebody's face in the glass, which you at first can't recognize as yourself. To unravel the bedquilt. To stop suddenly in that interesting occupation with a dim recollection that this action is mentioned in the medical books as the last fatal symptom of a declining patient.

When you have been in this way for a few days, a medical man will come to see you who will talk to you generally as if you were a "three-year child," and treat you as if he considered you an idiot. He will address his remarks to others rather than yourself, and occasionally ignore your presence entirely. His actions will leave the impression on your mind that he thinks you are averse to getting well, and must be coaxed or eventually coerced into a healthy condition. He will joke with you, perhaps, with such a palpable intention to make you laugh that you will feel like crying. He will call his powders "little," under the mistaken belief that they will be more acceptable. He will tell you that "we" must take care of "ourselves," and hand you something to make "us" sleep. This metaphorical sympathy with your condition will at first make you smile; but if you look at him closely and he be a clever man, you will see that this is simply a formula, and that under all there is a quiet watchfulness and quick perception, and meeting his eye at last you will understand one another, and you will like him better. If you subsequently get his good graces, he will tell you how all doctors have to fence with their patients, and may impart to you a few secrets of his trade which you think clergymen and lawyers might profit by.

If you are not so sick but that you can take your prescription to the chemist yourself, you will add something valuable to your experience. As you stand before the clean counter of the man of drugs, you will be able to detect, from the faces of the customers, which one is getting a prescription for himself. You will observe that in such cases the customer wears a look of anxiety and curiosity which he never has when a simple agent. You will yourself look narrowly at the bottles from which the druggist compounds your prescription, and if your knowledge of the Latin terminations be limited, you will be unnecessarily awed by their mysterious inscriptions. You will wonder if the druggist ever makes mistakes—if he ever puts up Sugar of Lead for Magnesia. You will perhaps meet one or two simple minded individuals, who will insist upon detailing their disorders to the druggist, as if it were to guide him in some mysterious way in the preparation of their prescriptions. But your prescription is ready, and as with the taking of medicine the psychological effects I have thus far recorded give way to mere physical phenomena, we find it convenient at this point to finish our record.   BRET.

CALIFORNIAN, *July* 22, 1865.

CHAPTER XIV

Complete Letter-Writing

T O WRITE an elegant letter has been usually considered a desirable accomplishment. Aids to this form of composition have been repeatedly offered to the public at prices, which, contrasted with the quality of moral sentiment and rhetorical elegance exhibited in the examples given for imitation, have seemed cheap indeed. For myself, although I am one of those who usually hang spellbound over a blank sheet of letter paper, and with difficulty sound their "dim perilous way" to a safe anchorage at the bottom of the sheet, I have availed myself but sparingly of these adventitious auxiliaries, and have a reasonable doubt whether this faculty of clever letter-writing can be called an accomplishment, or whether excellence therein is to be attained through precept and example. It is true that, in my youth, I was impressed with the history of a boy who wrote his mother a "beautiful letter," and who, said the chronicle, received a "plum cake" in reward. I fear that as an example the story was a signal failure. The general verdict of the juvenile circle of which I was a member, was that the epistolary youth was a prig—a verdict since sustained by my maturer judgment. Indeed, the only boy's-letter I ever thought worth reading was that which Mr. Charles Reade ascribes to Reginald Bazalgette, in one of his later novels—a letter hardly calculated to provoke a reward from the most indulgent parent. The question of what is really meritorious in this kind of composition remains unsettled, and also, whether beautiful letters, written with a more or less remote plum cake contingency, can be claimed to possess this virtue.

Every family possesses its "beautiful letter-writer," and nearly every family has some one member on whom the duty of correspondence mysteriously devolves, and who is looked upon as possessing a superior faculty. A critical analysis of the genius of this member, unfortunately, is very apt to disclose a preternatural tendency, on the part of that individual, to prolixity and verboseness, as well as the fact that his letters are not only too often insufferably stilted and vealy, but that they do not afford any index to the writer's real sentiments. The amount of moral and sentimental platitude that may be palmed off on one's relatives and friends in such cases is really wonderful. Enthusiastic uncles and cousins have been known to prefer their correspondent's description of notable events and occurrences—the correspondent evidently not shrinking from comparison—to those of the most clever professional writers, reading them to strangers with a perceptible mouthing and inordinate emphasis. This exalted praise sometimes results in the rash and premature appearance in print of the "beautiful" correspondent, where, by a system of compensation, he at once finds his level.

Disregard of sincerity and naturalness is the glory of most letter-writers. Two friends, accustomed to the free and simple interchange of thought, being separated, at once fall to filling pages of stilted formulæ—which neither accept as genuine—and to the bandying of fine epithets which they dare not, in ordinary circumstances, bring the tongue to pronounce. It is a knowledge of this propensity which sometimes adds a bitter pang to the parting of friends, each feeling dimly conscious that the other is destined to visit him hereafter as a prosy ghost, which he cannot exorcise. Each knows that the other will feel it necessary to philosophize and moralize in his new condition. Each will be astounded at depths of weaknesses hitherto unsuspected in each other's character. There is nothing so surely demonstrates this half consciousness of folly as the feeling with which we look over an old letter in the hands of a friend. "Is it possible that we wrote thus and so?" is the mental question that flushes our cheeks.

Our previous knowledge of a friend's character seldom affords us any indication of the tone of his letter. People are no more apt to write as we expect them to, than they are bound to act according to our comfortable predictions. Fanciful people very often write practical letters, and almost invariably the epistolary effusions of practical men abound in thin streaks of sentiment and poetry. Among a number of replies to a certain festive invitation, I once observed that the responses from clergymen were invariably the most jocular in intention—albeit somewhat too classical and heavy in execution. It will hardly be deemed probable that a D. D. should, in apologizing for his illness, allude to the possibility of his becoming "*clarior e* claret," yet such is the lamentable fact, and can be proven.

As there is a predisposition in the best of men to become bores at certain seasons, I look upon the attitude of epistolatory composition as alarmingly conducive to this weakness. With a blank sheet of paper before us, we hold our friends at a cruel disadvantage. We have it all our own way as we proceed to air our pet prejudices and hobbies; there is no one present to controvert, to yawn, to excuse himself, and we expand, we expiate, we become eloquent. Perhaps we have been accustomed to being snubbed in argument, and are quite willing to improve the occasion by letting our friend know that we too are a logician. I know of nothing so grimly humorous as the story told of our late good President and his patient attitude under the infliction of a wordy Pacific correspondent who, at last, broke him down with a letter of *seventy* pages. What a picture is offered in the spectacle of this homely rail-splitter whose reverent conscientiousness so sweetened his intercourse with his fellow-men that he achieved that miraculous courtesy which princes and peers have vainly cultivated.

What self-abnegation must have been employed in painfully winnowing the grain from all this chaff! Yet I confess I have not been without pity for the infelix epistolizer. Who can tell what dreary opinions on reconstruction, emancipation, and the Monroe doctrine were thus untimely cut off? Who knows what exhaustive and exhausting views of the resources of the Pacific slope were thus obscured? Who can speculate what histories of wrongs and rights and unrecognized merit were thus estopped? Whatever they were, the letter was never read, and yet by some unerring system of compensation, we know the correspondent only through the failure of that which might have kept him unknown.

Letters may be classified as the Business or practical, the Serious or sentimental, the Trifling or jocular. The characteristic of the business letter, legal or commercial, is to assert nothing that cannot be proven—hence this is perhaps the only kind of letter that is worth keeping. There are occasional combinations of this form of epistle, such as Serio-Business or the sentimental and practical letter—letters of condolence, lawyers' announcements of wills, and invitations to funerals and weddings. Indeed, it may be questioned whether all letters with a *motive* are not business letters. The sign of the Serious or sentimental is generally "Alas!" or the use of "'t were" for "it were," and inordinate poetical quotation. Any letter that begins with a description of scenery, the room in which the writer is sitting, a view from the window, or any allusion to the "setting sun," or other celestial phenomena, may be safely set down as belonging to this class. Remarks concerning the shortness of life, the vanity of human wishes, and all statements in regard to the soul, come under this head. A tendency to double epithets in the address, and a certain rhetorical flourish on approaching the signature, or a blending of the letter and signature, such as "the kindest regards of yours—" generally determine the sentimental form. The use of the word "epistle" for letter has a like significance. The Trifling or jocular is not as easily defined.

Any species of mild impertinence or garrulous imbecility, comes under this designation. Slang is perhaps its dominant characteristic. An idiotic use of quotation often constitutes the available capital of a "funny" letter-writer. Reputations for wit are built up in private families, on sentences like the following: " I feel like the 'Last Rose of Summer.' " "Write to me soon, for 'I'm lonely and forsaken.' " "Excuse mistakes, for I'm 'not meself at all.' " It is wonderful what thin potations suffice to intoxicate the social circle. I knew a gentleman whose letters were always received with what the newspaper critics call "shrieks of laughter." Yet the performances of this mad wag consisted in his occupying three sheets of letter-paper with his address and name.

If I were asked what I considered the highest form of epistolary excellence, I should say that, passing by those clever every-day working thoughts of men of genius, which often give us a better idea of their character than their more ambitious productions; passing by the quiet, simple and un-affected utterance of the educated gentleman whose self-poised reputation requires none of these adventitious aids to recognition, I would give the palm to the simplest letter of an honest gentlewoman. In it I should be confident of finding that sincerity and truthfulness without which the most courtly and elegant epistle is but sham and tinsel. In it I should find those instinctive truths which somehow come to the feminine mind as results without the trouble of their re-cording, as we do, the tedious processes. There is something beautiful and yet terrible in this frankness which invests every woman's letter. The thousand little artifices, coquetries and deceits which belong to their conversation vanish when they commit their white souls to the white paper. From the silliest school girl to the sedatest matron, disguise and digress how they may, the hidden secret, the true object, the real motive of their writing will pop out in every letter. It may be delayed as far as the postscript, but it is sure to come. It will be readily seen that this frankness is as perilous as it is charming. Perhaps I am not prepared to urge the passage of any statute forbidding young women to write, and denying them postal facilities, and it is highly probable that if such were the law they would find some equally dangerous avenue of expression; but this would not and should not prevent those of our own sex who may have become the recipients of these dangerous confidences from guarding them as sacredly as their own honor. If I were the mentor of any young lady-killer, I would advise him to burn his *billet-doux*, however sweet, promising that if he did not receive his reward in the self-consciousness of a virtuous and manly action, he would at least find his correspondence greatly increased when the fact became known. BRET.

CALIFORNIAN, *August* 19, 1865.

CHAPTER XV

𝔄 𝔅ook for the 𝔗imes

I N V I E W of the requirements of the advanced civilization on this coast, and the necessity of polite text-books and indigenous rules for social and elegant intercourse, THE CALIFORNIAN offers the following extracts from a new work shortly to be issued from this office, entitled:

THE CALIFORNIAN
COMPLETE LETTER WRITER

No. 1. *From a Mining Secretary*

DEAR SIR.—You are hereby advised that, in consequence of delinquent assessments, ten (10) shares in the Dedbilque Mining Company, standing in your name, were yesterday *sold*.

Yours, etc.,   JOHN JONES, Secretary.

———

No. 2. *From a Stockholder*

DEAR SIR.—I am in receipt of your communication stating that in consequence of delinquent assessments ten (10) shares of the Dedbilque Mining Company, standing in my name, were yesterday *sold*. In reply, I would state that the shares seem to have followed the example of the shareholder.

I am yours,   JOHN BROWN.

———

No. 3. *From a Guardian*

MY DEAR SNIGSBY.—I arrived yesterday per steamer from the East, having in charge your intended bride. The voyage was an exceedingly pleasant one. I found the lady all that your glowing fancy painted. Thoroughly convinced of the correctness of your taste and judgment, and yielding to her delicate instincts, which revolted at receiving protection from one who was not a relative, I proposed, was accepted, and married her myself on the passage up. This will account for the non-appearance of her name on the passenger-list. I enclose cards; also, a draft on you for her passage money, as per agreement.

Very truly, your friend,   BREEZY COOL.

No. 4. From an Editor to a Poet

DEAR SIR.—I have received your letter in which you state "you enclose a Poem," and offer a proposition for its publication. As I am unable yet to accede to the first of your propositions, I cannot enter into a consideration of the second.

I am yours, etc.   JEFFERSON BRICK.

No. 5. From a Lad at Boarding School to his Father in the City

DEAR FATHER.—I am getting on very finely with my studies, and the second Punic war occurred shortly after the death of Augustus, and in consequence of the defections of Aristophanes. The distance from the earth to the sun is over fifty billions of miles, and if you fired a shot from a cannon, it would take twenty thousand years to reach it. It is also slightly flattened at the poles. Dear Father, I swapped with Bill Fisher my watch for ten shares in the Jupiter Gammon Mining Company, and want you to send me some money to pay assessments. All the boys went to see a bull-fight last Saturday, but I stayed in. It is wrong to see bull-fights when you have no money to go in.

Your affectionate son,   THOMAS.

CHAPTER XVI

Railway Reading

SHORT stories that combine a certain amount of sentiment with a catastrophe sufficiently thrilling, have been invariably found acceptable to the travelling reader. A plot not so intricate as to interfere with the observation of scenery; a sentiment not so exalted as to be incompatible with flirtation or the chewing of spruce gum or lozenges, have been usually considered specially fit for this style of romance. Magazines, weekly papers, and "Dime Novels" have provided this literary reflection for the weary traveller. For the mind as well as the body requires refreshment, and if it comes in that crude and indigestible shape usually so fatal to the traveller's stomach, it is excusable as one of the exigencies of travel.

Of late years the character of these stories has alarmingly changed. The fascinating hero and stately heroine whose fortunes we breathlessly followed in the railway carriage or steamboat cabin, have passed away. Let us recall the almost invariable conditions under which they made their appearance. The scenery was usually foreign—the *dramatis personæ* noble. Can we forget the ingenious youth, who in humble circumstances, yet bearing about him an "indescribable air" of being somebody, snubbed one of "England's proudest peers," triumphantly married the daughter of an Earl, and, after asserting the dignity of simple manhood—O, fatal *lapsus*—proved in the last chapter to be "the rightful heir and the noblest blood in the kingdom." Perhaps there is no better evidence of the innate snobbery of our sympathies than this very common *denouement*. Forged wills—which by a careful observation of romances seem to comprise seven-eighths of all the wills made—liberal quotations from the French, and language which if not always grammatical, was invariably beautiful, lent a fascinating interest to the romance. On this moving picture of high life and its attendant sympathies, the conductor's request to see the reader's ticket—a request which always implies a certain degree of suspicion—broke all too harshly.

When the short-story writer laid his plot nearer home we could not help feeling that his genius was cramped. Yet how masterly the manner in which the American Indian—almost as imperfectly understood as the English nobleman—was handled in those pages. What flowers of rhetoric surrounded the picturesque savage. How perfectly satisfied we were to believe that he invariably addressed us in the abstract, as "the Pale Face," that he seldom spoke three consecutive sentences without an allusion to the "Great Spirit," that his daughter was a model of womanly grace and beauty. Again, the American Revolution was a fruitful source of inspiration to the story-writer of twenty years ago. What liberties were taken with the events of that historic epoch! Were we ever mysteriously introduced to a "tall, commanding figure," and "face of great dignity and benevolence" without instantly recognizing George Washington? The private matters in which "the Father of his Country" personally interfered, the love affairs which he conducted to a successful termination, would alone seem to justify his reputation. How often did the genial face of Israel Putnam beam upon us from those pages; how quickly did we recognize Francis Marion, who has passed in some mysterious way into history as perpetually exciting the astonishment of British officers on the subject of his diet and domestic economy? Nor were the domestic virtues neglected by the short-story writers. Mildly interesting

stories of three or four chapters in length, the plot laid in a
New England village—a dark hint of reality conveyed by the
initials of some of the principal characters such as "Judge
L.," "Squire B.," and "Deacon O.," were very popular at
that period. The heroine usually died early; wasting away
under the combined effect of fancy fairs, singing schools,
donation parties, social teas, and other local excitements.
Upon this gloomy peroration did the short-story writer lavish
the wealth of his rhetoric. Not content with an affecting
description of her death-bed, he evidently took a gloomy
satisfaction in the details of her funeral, not did he dismiss us
without the information that "in the lovely little village of
D." "a simple slab in the country churchyard" was all that
preserved "the memory of Mary B." Perhaps it is unnecessary to say that this was in the "spring tide"—a season
peculiarly fatal to romantic loveliness.

The different reforms and philanthropic enterprises of out
country were also favorable to the genius of the short-story
writer. Without alluding to the efforts of that great Master
of American Moral Fiction—Mr. T. S. Arthur—a romantic
Poor Richard engrafted upon a prose Tupper—what reader
has forgotten the young mechanic who drank a single glass of
wine at an evening party, and thereby involved himself and
family in general ruin; the young couple who laid aside three
cents a day and ultimately attained wealth and respectability, the husband dying an Assemblyman; the young
woman who lost the affection of her lover—an eligible young
man, for the writer never lost sight of the practical in the
romantic—through a single pettish word; the young wife who
dressed too much; the slatternly wife who didn't dress
enough— But why continue? Are not these things still written in the book of Godey—the magazine of Peterson?

The change which has come over the romantic dreams of
the short-story writer has been slow but insidious. The heroine whose stateliness we loved, has become arch, vivacious,
and witty to a painful degree. Instead of thrilling us with that

melancholy glance which was supposed to express in some orthodox manner "the yearnings of a poetic soul" she now transfixes us with a sarcasm. Instead of those conversations magnificent in hyperbole and lofty in sentiment, we have now badinage that becomes almost hysterical in its intensity. Her head no longer sinks on her lover's manly breast, as she "whispers sweet consent"—"a sudden expression almost of pain"—"a cold rigidity of the small lips"—"a mocking, but silvery laugh" is all that the bashful lover may look for. Not but that she has sentiment, but it is of a singularly perplexing and exasperating quality—she has a way of looking at you "with strange dumb eyes"—her glance is "trance like," and "far off"—she is "sybilline," "fateful." She is no longer beautiful, but "singular looking." It may be easily imagined that a heroine of this order would not be satisfied with that one devoted lover which in former times was her predestined partner. She loves two. She is two or three times engaged. She is justified by a philosophy borrowed from our lively Gallic friends. She has all the benefit of those "extenuating circumstances" which French poetical justice admits equally as its literature and law. The modern short story gives us details, where formerly we had mere glittering generalities. The dress of our heroine is described with feminine precision; the writer no longer trusts to white muslin and "simple rosebuds" for the hair. In the matter of accomplishments the same care is displayed. Our heroine no longer allows her fingers to run carelessly over the piano while she listens to her lover's conversation; she deliberately sits down to Chopin or Schubert. We are forced to listen to an enthusiastic criticism of "Beethoven, choral symphony op. 125," or a "duo in E flat." We are crushed with her knowledge of botany; the "simple rosebud" her lover presents is technically considered; it is no longer pulled to pieces in bashful meditation —she "removes its petals." In the more pretentious short-story, she generally has a profession—painter, musician, sculptor, governess, doctor. The hero—at best, the male of

her species—is absorbed in her superior attractions. He is no
longer young; middle-aged heroes are naturally much more
fascinating to the female short story writers of a certain age.
He is fascinatingly rough and out-spoken in manner; he is
satirical and philosophical; he is learned and ponderous. His
voice is deep-toned; his grasp is hearty; he is kind even in his
rudeness. In fact, the feminine idea of man would seem to be
generally based on a study of Newfoundland dogs and mas-
tiffs. Perhaps he is a soldier—an Union officer—but this
supposition opens such an exhausting and illimitable view of
hospitals with sick nurses, battlefields, politics, and wounded
soldiers returning with high honors—and the countless
romances of the civil war which have taken the place of the
old Revolutionary episodes, that we must needs pause.

Of such stuff are the heroes and heroines of the modern
short-stories made. We meet them in the pages of the magazine or weekly that we glance over in the railway car or
steamboat; we are more or less interested in their fate or fortune, but they are apt to pass out of our minds with the
vanishing objects that we hurry past. For the short-story is
not a matter of deliberate reading—nor does it exact the attitude of attention and complete abstraction. What is written
here of course does not refer to the lighter efforts of the few
great romancers of our day, nor the really clever sketches—
not stories—of English periodicals, which develop humor and
satire, rather than plot or incident. And yet an age which puts
into our hands the latest chapters of the great serial writers,
as we walk or ride; which gives us cheap pocket editions of
our noblest poets; which collates for our hurried recreation in
review or eclectic all that is good of refined and epicurean
literature; which enables us to delight in the pathos or humor
of simple duty as sketched by master hands, instead of the
forced and unnatural romance of the sentimental hack, surely
offers us some compensation for the gradual decay of short-
story telling. It is certainly something to be thankful for that
our wives and daughters travelling by land or sea are more

likely to refresh themselves with books whose pages breathe
an atmosphere as pure, as fresh, and as wholesome as that
which blows through the open window, than in the days when
literature spread its refreshment table for the weary traveller
with indigestible moral pie, sensational hot coffee, sentimental tea, and emotional soda water.   BRET.

CALIFORNIAN, *June* 9, 1866.

CHAPTER XVII

On the Sagacity of the Newfoundland

THE HIGH intellectual qualities which Cuvier, Buffon and Goldsmith agree in attributing to the Newfoundland, I am satisfied, do but scant justice to the mental capacity of that sagacious animal. The point, I believe, usually made in his favor, is his habit of plunging into the water and rescuing people from drowning, but, as I have frequently had occasion to observe that he exhibits an equal solicitude for sticks and stones, or, indeed, anything that his master may first spit upon, and then throw overboard, I do not think that the intellectual quality of the habit is conclusively proven. I am so well satisfied of this, that I feel confident that my dog—albeit an unusually intelligent member of the species—would refuse through logical consistency to rescue even my most intimate friends, unless they had first been spat upon and thrown in by me.

Nevertheless, although I point with pride to the fact that nobody has been drowned at my residence on Bush street since his advent in the family, I base the evidences of his intellect on somewhat higher grounds. He early evinced a disposition to attack passing Chinamen. I should have probably overlooked this circumstance, had not my attention been previously attracted to an editorial in one of the daily papers conclusively proving the inferiority of the Mongolian race, and I at once saw that what I had presumed to be simply a brutal instinct, was really a mental effort of considerable ability. I have seen him bark at an inoffensive John with a persistency that was as offensive if not as convincing, as a column of rhetoric. I have seen him pursue negroes with that

fine blending of ferocity and intelligence which I have hitherto supposed to be peculiar to the *genus homo*. When I have
watched him *flush*—if I may so call it—a bevy of colored
children on their way to schoo and stand with his handsome
head erect, his silken ears slightly raised at their bases, his
tail lightly tossing like a martial plume—uttering deep-
mouthed protests against this manifest abuse of the educa-
tional system, he has seemed to me to be an embodiment of
chivalrous and aristocratic breeding.

In regard to his literary habits, of which no mention is
made by Buffon or other naturalists, I would now speak. My
attention was first drawn to the fact by his abusive attitude
toward the carrier of a certain newspaper, at whom he con-
tinually growled. Although this first attempt at criticism was
abstract and vague, he eventually improved upon it so much
as to separate the irresponsible agent from the distasteful
object itself, and spent his animosity upon the paper. This
he literally "chewed up." During the term of my subscrip-
tion, I do not think that an entire copy of the journal ever
reached me; there was usually a column, a page or a paragraph missing. Nor were these objectionable features of the
paper apparently confined to the editorial expression; very
frequently whole columns of advertisements were the subject
of his displeasure. To the savageness he also added the im-
personality of the critic; he never permitted himself to be
caught in the act, but always wore an air of quiet unconsciousness, when his conduct was the subject of comment,
that never revealed his complicity. A few days after this a
copy of some Congressional speech was missing from my
desk, and was found in the garden, having been clandestinely
purloined by him. A preternaturally uninteresting tract, and
one or two pamphlets—one, I think, on the cholera—soon
followed. Had he occupied himself with this lighter kind of
mental pabulum, I should not possibly have interfered. But
when his taste for knowledge extended to bound volumes—
when a copy of Pope, vilely handled, was found on the veran-

dah—I found it necessary to correct him. He subsequently took Lamb and Bacon, but, as an ingenious young friend assured me that this was evidently through a too literal conception of their titles, I excused him. But when this same young person attempted to justify the seizure of Hogg's Tales as an act not inconsistent with the dog's previous habits, I could only look upon the hypothesis as pleasing in its verbal felicity, but inaccurate in its logic.

That quality of discriminating intelligence which, according to the Ethiopian belief, keeps the monkey from talking lest he should be made to work, was exhibited to a high degree by my Newfoundland. My attempts to teach him certain useful tricks failed solely through his extraordinary sagacity. When I offered him a basket to carry, he would wag his tail and otherwise shew his perfect understanding of the service required, but firmly and quietly decline the office. When I ordered him to go out, he would walk as far as the threshold to show his comprehension of the order, and return to his post on the hearth-rug, to show his superior knowledge of the comparative merits of the two places. He always helped himself, when unobserved, to the victual reserved for the table, in preference to that set apart for his own use, with a fine discrimination of quality. When I sometimes found it necessary to urge him to attack strange dogs which infested our garden —if he hesitated and exhibited a desire to bark at them from the parlor windows—if he preferred vocal abuse to prompt and physical action—I generally found that the dogs were larger than himself, and that his decision was the result of reason rather than instinct. So well am I satisfied of his sagacity that I am convinced he only waits an opportunity to find some more comfortable lodgings to desert mine, and far from imitating the mere animal instinct which governed Ulysses' dog, I am satisfied that if, in the mysterious future I should present myself as a beggar to him, he would at once recognize my descent in the social scale, and unhesitatingly attack me.   BRET.

CHAPTER XVIII

Outcroppings and Tailings

UTCROPPINGS. being selections of California verse, was a book arranged and edited by Bret Harte. It brought forth such a storm of adverse criticism from the jealous partisans of local poets not included, that Bret Harte wrote two witty and satirical reviews of an imaginary book, "Tailings, being rejections of California verse." Of course, THE CALIFORNIAN championed Bret Harte and his selections and the battle was on. The following reviews were taken from THE CALIFORNIAN.—EDITOR.

NEW BOOKS

We are indebted to A. Roman & Co., No. 417 and 419 Montgomery street, for the following new books:

[1]*Outcroppings; being Selections of California Verse.* A. Roman & Co., San Francisco.

That a publisher should publish, at his own expense, a volume of selections from California newspaper poetry, is, perhaps, the most remarkable feature of this volume. The climate and material character of California civilization are not favorable to the development of the poetical faculty, notwithstanding the grandeur and sublimity of local scenery—a fact which the compiler seems to have confessed, in perfect simplicity, but which does not seem to have deterred him, as it should, from issuing such a work. In a community so small, and where there are so few poets whose literary merit is

---

[1]Compiled by Bret Harte. He wrote the introduction to the book, but according to his friend Webb, none of his own poems appear in it.—EDITOR.

definitely established, any preference or selection must always seem invidious, and is not only an exercise of grave responsibility, but is a decision always open to appeal, as the expression of a single individual mind. Who is the compiler does not appear; it is hinted that he has written verses himself, and, if we may follow the natural tendencies of the poetic disposition, it would be fair to seek him among those who are most prominently represented in this volume.

CALIFORNIAN, *December 9, 1865.*

INIGOINGS

SAN FRANCISCO, Friday, December 15th, 1865.

The population of California is now divided into two classes: Those who contributed to *Outcroppings* and those who did not.

The latter have decidedly the advantage, so far as number is concerned. Merit, I think, is pretty evenly divided.

For my part, I think there is something better in life than to be an Outcropper.

A better title for the book could not have been found, for a good many croppings are left out—out in the cold, so to speak.

I have looked for "The Prophetess," but she is not there. Why is this thus? as Artemus Ward says.

Have prophetesses no honor in their own country, as well as prophets?

One of the house of Roman remarked, when I commented upon finding no prophetess in the book, that he didn't see much profit there either.

It grieves me to think that among so many singers the seat of one should be vacant—was there no room in the Pitt?

My opinion is that in making his selections, the editor's aim was to select the worst verse the State afforded—and he has succeeded admirably. Indeed, the title would so indicate; for what are outcroppings but rough surface rock?

I notice that the editor put none of his own compositions in the volume—making a feint of modesty. May we not say to him? "feint, Harte, never won fair lady."

By the way, Christmas is coming. It has been coming for some time, but it is nearer now than it was a while ago.

And I am ready to receive presents.

I don't mean that I want anybody to send me poems—they would be called instances of presents of mind, I suppose; but no one need mind about sending me any.

I already have a volume of *Outcroppings*, and that is nearly as much as one crop can stand.

But diamonds, jewelry, vases, corner lots, coal-scuttles—anything neat, ornamental, and valuable, will be gratefully received by   INIGO.

CALIFORNIAN, *December* 23, 1865.

A NEW CALIFORNIA BOOK, TAILINGS

[REVIEWED BY THE CALIFORNIAN'S CONDENSED NOVELIST]

Tailings; being rejections of California Verse. Seventeen vols., 8mo. Gold Hill: *Daily News* Publishing Company. Virginia City: *Daily Enterprise.* Whiskey Creek: *Sentinel.*

This exquisite work, published simultaneously by the *Daily Enterprise*, the Gold Hill *Daily News* and the Whiskey Creek *Sentinel*, makes not only a valuable but a considerable addition to any library. It is an offset to the manifest unfairness of a volume lately issued by Roman & Co., entitled *Outcroppings*, and contains all the productions rejected from that volume, through the ignorance, presumption and prejudice of the compiler. In contradistinction to *Outcroppings*, not only the editorship but the contents of this volume are personal; and far from omitting their own productions, through hypocritical modesty, the contributions of the editor alone occupy twelve of the seventeen volumes.

Those who are familiar with the peculiar imagery which distinguishes the editorials of the Virginia *Enterprise* will recognize the following gem:

SUNRISE ON MT. DAVIDSON

[BY THE EDITOR OF THE ENTERPRISE]

Lo! where the orient hills are tipped with snow,
The pregnant morn slow waddles o'er the plain,
Big with the coming day; the shameless child
Of Erebus and Nox, wrought in the slow
And sure gestation of the rolling hours.
How great is the fecundity of Time!
Methinks I see the swaddling clothes of mist
Roll down the bosky glens, and standing here
Note book in hand, I really seem to be
Accoucher of the Universe.

                             Oh, go
And bag your heads, ye shameless bards, whose weak
Conceptions are abortions! Let me hie
Where the soft strains of hurdy-gurdies call
And fair Teutonic maidens do invite
To shades of yonder cellar; there to con
From Holleck, Dunglison, and Matsell's sheet,
Chaste figures for my fancy, ere perchance
The printer call for copy.

Two or three poems by the lamented Jayhawk—whose grand description of the Sierras are superior even to the grandeur of the mountains themselves—find a place in this volume. The "Lines to Hank Monk" are exquisitely beautiful, and the sonnets to the "Summit House" and "Strawberry," equal, if not surpass, Coleridge's "Hymn in the Vale of Chamouni." It is to be regretted that an unpleasant altercation respecting the proprietorship of a watch and some money, which occurred on a dark night during the temporary stoppage of the Overland Stage, should have resulted in this promising young man's untimely decease.

A few fine maledictory stanzas addressed to the compiler of *Outcroppings*, a beautiful idyl entitled "Go and Bag Your Head," and an elegiac poem on the editor of the *Enterprise*, are among the gems contributed by the Gold Hill *News*. We are tempted to give a single stanza of the latter:

> "Bold chieftain with the vitreous eye,
>   Old stallion of the land of Storey!
> Shall dastard Flop-tods make thee fly,
>   Or purp-stuff dim thine ancient glory;
> No—leave the hurdy-gurdy halls—
>   The maidens fair that would scuyugle,
> Ha! Ha! the foe before thee falls,
>   Smashed by a paster on the bugle!"

A Friend of the Rejected contributes a fine poem, addressed to the editor of *Outcroppings*, apparently modelled after, but far superior to Mr. Emerson's "Brahma," commencing: "If the compiler thinks he's safe." Every one will admire the Doric simplicity of the following verse:

> "They reckon ill who leave me out,
>   When me they fly—I clip their wings,
> I am that self-same Richard Doubt,
>   Of whom the Nursery maiden sings."

Equally beautiful is the poem by the editor of the Grass Valley *National*, entitled "The Pi-Ute." We make room for a few stanzas. The double rhyme in the first verse has an effect of startling beauty:

> "Gleaming with silver and alkali,
> The barren plains of Nevada lie.
> Over them glides with stealthy foot
> The crouching form of the bold Pi-Ute.
> Three-toed Jim, and one-eyed Nick,
> Dusty Jake, and Slippery Dick,
> Wah-no-tee, and O-kee chee,
> Muck-a-Muck and Su-mar-kee."

Then follows a graphic description of the gathering of the tribes and a beautiful portrayal of morning in the miner's camp:

> "And through the valleys rose between
> The pleasant hiss of the esculent bean,
> And the jay bird's thrilling song was stopped,
> When the luscious flap-jack softly flopped."

But our confined space forbids further extracts. We expect to enrich our columns from time to time with excerpts from this charming work. We may briefly notice two fine poems of the Sacramento *Union*, entitled "Inland Domesticity Ignorant of the Cosmopolitan Sea," after A. Pike, and an epic of the "Gold-Hunting Crusade," beginning with the escapade of the Stevenson Regiment from the sheriff of New York, and ending with the first Vigilance Committee. A local item from *Alta California* is admitted by the compiler on the ground that it was not *prose*. We understand that 1,280 copies are already spoken for—by a singular coincidence, being the exact number of rejected poets. The work is handsomely bound and printed on tinted litmus paper.

CALIFORNIAN, *December 23*, 1865.

TAILINGS*, SECOND NOTICE

[BY "BRET," THE CALIFORNIAN'S CONDENSED REVIEWER]

It is with considerable satisfaction that we again recur to this truly admirable collection of the poetry of our Golden State. It is a work eminently Californian—and having said that, what more need be said? Freed from the enfeebling restraints which an older and more cultivated civilization throws around its bards; following no blind precedent of grammatical, metrical or rhythmical construction, our poets in this volume may be truly said to have made "a law with themselves." We believe, with the Sacramento *Union*, that the natural advantages of California are provocative of the grandest poesy, and that the Sierras of our State as surely tend to the creation of poets as the Alps of Switzerland do the propagation of *cretins* and idiots. If the compiler of *Outcroppings* had, instead of following Eastern precedent, looked through nature and the interior press, he would have spared himself the just designation of a "pitiful ass," which the *Sunday Mercury*, with a singular precision of epithet, so truly applies to him. We may remark, incidentally, that the notices of the interior press and the few city papers which reflect the provincial tone, are, with but one exception, unanimous in these flattering notices. The *Sunday Mercury* says: "In looking over this work we cannot help reflecting the words of the Grecian poet, *Parturient montes nascitur non fit*. It is a magnificent monument of human labor and skill, as enduring as the pyramids of the Eternal City; its editor is unquestionably a genius, while the compiler of *Outcroppings* is a d—n fool!" The Gold Hill *News* characteristically but playfully remarks: "No hog-wash or purp-stuff here—the real Helicon, unmixed with slumgullion." The single exception to the tenor of these notices we find in the columns of the *Fiddletown Skirmisher:* "A degrading and dastardly attempt," says that journal, "to rob H. J. Sedilia, so long a contributor to our columns, of his just claims to immortality, has been made by the publishers of *Tailings*. Without him the work is bosh!"

As we turn to the pages of the *Tailings* we find the following gem, which may be justly considered superior to Tennyson's "Eagle":

THE JAYHAWK

He grasps the swag with hooking hand,
He sees the stage come overland,
Serene in ambush doth he stand.

The toiling team below him crawls,
He looketh from his mountain walls,
And like a thunderbolt he falls.

He falleth on the good and just,
Their heads he grindeth in the dust,
And then he busteth in their crust!

Among the fugitive pieces, readers of the *Bulletin* will recognize the following stanzas addressed to "A Fashionable Church" by an Honest Miner. We give the two first verses:

As I gaze on yon church with its porches so grand,
   And its towers so tall and so steep,
I think of the earthquake that one day will shake
   Its walls to a moldering heap,
               And weep
   For the harvest these wretches shall reap.

O yes, you may build your disgusting old fane,
   And say to your heart, it is well;
But I look below its foundations and know
   That underneath that there is hell—
               And smell
   The sulphurous odors that dwell.

But we cannot consistently admire the line which seems to have been superadded, in its present grammatical inaccuracy:

               And yell
   With delight when the whole shanty fell.

After inveighing against pride and vanity, the poet concludes somewhat vaguely:

And one-half the world will be damned if they don't,
   And the other half damned if they do—
               And you,
   Proud palace of error, adieu!

The influence of Tennyson on the provincial mind is beautifully and tenderly shewn in the following:

ONE HORSE FLAT

Pard'ner, leave me here a moment; leave me here and go before;
Leave me here, and while you're absent I'll prospect a little more.

'Tis the place and there's the pine tree where of old the squirrels sat,
Dreary gleams the white quartz tailings lying over One Horse Flat.

One Horse Flat, that in the distance overlooks the Stanislow,
And the Chinese on the river kicking up a bloody row.

O, my claim too long forgotten! O my tunnel, mine no more!
O, the empty, empty ditches, and the rock devoid of ore

In the Spring there comes a blossom on the nose of every Pike,
In the Spring a young man fancies he is sure to make a strike.

In the Spring he lightly gambles, drawing on his future means,
In the Spring he holds two aces, and he bucks agin three queens.

Bill took up the dice and shook 'em with a sweet seraphic smile,
Shook the dice and threw four sixes, and of course raked down the pile.

But he dealt the keerds more deftly than was fit in one so young,
And my eyes on all his motions with a mute observance hung.

And I said, "My festive William, speak and speak the truth to me:
How it is when I've two aces, that thou always dost have three?"

Then he turned, his whole cheek flushing—he was taken by surprise—
With a quiet imprecation in regard to his own eyes.

Saying: "I have hid the bower, Pard'ner—I would do thee wrong,
And my boots the king and ten-spot have been holding all along."

Many an evening in our cabin did we sit with flaring dips,
And the spirits mixed together, that we tasted with our lips.

Many an evening with a neighbor did we turn the festive Jack,
Lightly dealt ourselves the bowers from the bottom of the pack.

But why continue the old, old story of misplaced confidence and violated trust. The poet was deceived by his partner, and, in a single game of cut-throat euchre, lost the whole of his claim. Stung by disappointment, he announces his intention to go to Washoe, which is beautifully described as being an

> "Oasis of sage brush lying in a field of alkali,"

and affiliate with some Digger squaw:

> "I will take some dusky savage for my partner, and I'll eat
> The succulent grasshopper, and the luscious locust meat."

But we find ourselves beguiled beyond our usual space. Let our readers purchase the volume and judge for themselves. Agents are now engaged in selling the work in connection with Mrs. Winslow's Soothing Syrup. Price, one set of "Tailings" and one bottle of the syrup, $1.50. A rare chance for investment.

Tailings: being Rejections of California Verse.

CALIFORNIAN, *December 30*, 1865.

If you will compare "The Heathen Chinee" on the following pages with the poem, "One Horse Flat" on the preceding pages you will see a marked similarity of diction, names and general situation. This similarity has led us to believe that 'One Horse Flat" contains the nucleus of the idea of "The Heathen Chinee" published five years later. For a fuller comparison of the two poems see page XVIII of the preface to The New Edition.—EDITOR.

PLAIN LANGUAGE FROM TRUTHFUL JAMES

Table Mountain, 1870

Which I wish to remark—
    And my language is plain—
That for ways that are dark
    And for tricks that are vain,
The heathen Chinee is peculiar.
    Which the same I would rise to explain.

Ah Sin was his name;
    And I shall not deny
In regard to the same
    What that name might imply,
But his smile it was pensive and child-like,
    As I frequent remarked to Bill Nye.

It was August the third;
    And quite soft was the skies;
Which it might be inferred
    That Ah Sin was likewise;
Yet he played it that day upon William
    And me in a way I despise.

Which we had a small game,
    And Ah Sin took a hand:
It was Euchre. The same
    He did not understand;
But he smiled as he sat by the table,
    With the smile that was child-like and bland.

Yet the cards they were stocked
    In a way that I grieve,
And my feelings were shocked
    At the state of Nye's sleeve:
Which was stuffed full of aces and bowers,
    And the same with intent to deceive.

But the hands that were played
    By that heathen Chinee,
And the points that he made,
    Were quite frightful to see—
Till at last he put down a right bower,
    Which the same Nye had dealt unto me.

Then I looked up at Nye,
   And he gazed upon me;
And he rose with a sigh,
   And said "Can this be?
We are ruined by Chinese cheap labor"—
   And he went for that heathen Chinee.

In the scene that ensued
   I did not take a hand,
But the floor it was strewed
   Like the leaves on the strand
With the cards that Ah Sin had been hiding,
   In the game "he did not understand."

In his sleeves, which were long,
   He had twenty-four packs—
Which was coming it strong,
   Yet I state but the facts;
And we found on his nails, which were taper
   What is frequent in tapers—that's wax.

Which is why I remark,
   And my language is plain,
That for ways that are dark,
   And for tricks that are vain,
The heathen Chinee is peculiar—
   Which the same I am free to maintain.

Reprinted from the original issue in the Overland monthly, September, 1870.—EDITOR.

A SHEAF OF CRITICISM

In a recent review of *Outcroppings*, THE CALIFORNIAN intimated that the volume would probably provoke some criticism, which would definitely settle a standard by which the efforts of California poets should be judged. That intimation has proven but partially correct; a few criticisms have been made, but they do not materially affect this question. It is nothing that we hear of representative poems and representative poets—every clique, every village, has its one predestined genius—if we are offered as yet no valid reason for according them a position.

Yet we confess to be somewhat concerned at the alarming shape some of these criticisms have taken. We cannot help feeling as though we were in some way concerned in precipitating them upon the head of the infelix compiler. We observe that the detached names of poets are thrown at him a good deal in the manner of epithets, and that he is pelted with fragments of verses, as though they were decayed cabbages—a resemblance not entirely inconsistent with their material. It would seem that "the air was full of poets"—that the gods overflow the California Pantheon, and that, owing to the crowded condition of the Washoe Valhalla, her immortals have been obliged to fulminate from lager beer cellars.

The nearest approximation to proper criticism has appeared in the *California Leader* over the signature of "Mufti." As it is partly addressed to THE CALIFORNIAN, and as it is written in the urban rather than the provincial style, we cheerfully give it precedence in this review. But the article is unfinished; the remainder is promised this week, and we are unable to judge how far its present incompleteness is the result of accident. The writer tells us frankly that his criticism is partly in answer to a friend who, in conversation, rashly ascribed superior critical qualities to THE CALIFORNIAN. As this is the clearest statement in the entire article, we cannot help congratulating this friend, although we suspect him to be a masculine Mrs. Harris, and a near relation of one Bliebenicht, with whom "Mufti" is in the habit of holding imaginary conversations, on his escape from the indefinite length of that critical dissertation, which Mufti seems to have commenced as to a friend, but to have continued as to an enemy.

We were prepared for a review in the *Territorial Enterprise*, for the *Gold Hill News*, after playfully alluding to the obnoxious volume as "purp-stuff," intimated that the editor of the *Enterprise* had written superior poems. But we were not prepared for four columns and a-half of a review to prove what was apparent in his first paragraph, that he was one of the neglected poets. There is no doubt that the circumstance was aggravating, and that the editor exhibits a certain fire and agility in his review. But it is the Fire of St. Anthony—it is the Dance of St. Vitus. The poetic and the scrofulous temperaments are analogous—high spirits and brilliancy are too often simply the exaltation of fever. The editor loses his temper, and calls the compiler bad names. He intimates that he is a coward and a hypocrite—but that he is not a coward because he is a hypocrite—and ergo that he is not a hypocrite, because he is a coward. He permits himself to indulge in a most extraordinary illustration, which we cannot, in decency, repeat in these columns. And yet, after a simile, which is a curious commingling of the language of obstetrics and the *National Police Gazette*, he speaks of a certain poet as having an *unclean* imagination. We do not know what is the popular form of imagery in Virginia City, or what is considered clean, but if the editor of the *Enterprise* writes for an audience beyond those classic precincts, we beg him, in spite of the advice of the compiler, *not* "to look in his own heart" for his "imagery," or "in the fortunes of his fellow men." He gives us a vision of "blue fire and lurid flames," but, as the confession of such experiences is usually confined to tracts on intemperance, we think it a little out of place in a book review. But we have an idea that he is already as ashamed of his passion as he is of his logic, which assumes for its premises what he *believes* other people *think*, or his critical acumen, which applies the epithet "rollicking" to the Keats-like verse of Stoddard, and we trust that he will hereafter remember that the functions of a critic and the qualities of a gentleman are not inconsistent.

We are charmed at the ingenuity with which the Sacramento *Union* makes the review of this book an opportunity to raise the familiar song of self-laudation and California egoism which has brought our newspaper literature to ridicule in Eastern circles. If the finely turned rhetoric of its opening paragraph be offered as a specimen of California descriptive poetry, we think that the compiler of *Outcroppings* has made a mistake in his covert sneer at the California pastorals. But as the *Union* recapitulates the many poetical provocations of the California existence, which must read like the counts of a ferocious indictment to the *wretched writer of that preface, some of its details are vague. It instances, as one of the compelling causes to poetry, "inland domesticity, ignorant of the cosmopolitan sea." In our editorial capacity we have read a good many poems, evidently the product of "inland domesticity," but whether or not accompanied by obliviousness "to the cosmopolitan sea," we are at a loss to determine. If this be a polite periphrasis for those who have "come across the plains," we think the *Union* is correct. Phœnix's "He was Accidentally Shot," and Mark Twain's "He Done his Level Best," are fair instances of the poetical tendencies of "inland domesticity ignorant of the cosmopolitan sea," and certainly have been wrongfully overlooked in the volume. The *Union* believes that the "grand gold hunting crusade" would make a fine theme for epic. We are inclined to think it would. Something in the style of the episode of the *Argonautœ*, with Sam Brannan for "Jason," Michael Reese for "Theseus," and the editor of the *Union* as the "Orpheus" who sings the romantic chronicle. And it may be that here we shall find what is considered the true California standard of poetical taste—that which is most Californian.

*Note.—Assuredly all by Bret Harte himself. Who else would dare to say "the wretched writer of that preface."—EDITOR.

CALIFORNIAN, *December* 23, 1865.

OUTCROPPINGS COME AGAIN

On another page we republish all the notices of *Outcroppings* which reach us through the columns of Eastern exchanges. The *Bulletin*, with that courtesy and generosity which have made it the favorite of its contemporaries and its proprietors so popular among men, has spared us the trouble of reproducing any of the vituperations which have been written on this coast, by giving up its own columns to their republication. This was scarcely, however, a work of love so much as of necessity, for the dead blank left where the telegraphic news was formerly found must be filled. Consequently no special obligations are expressed or implied on either side.

As a general thing it may be said of the criticisms thus embalmed in the amber of the *Bulletin's* columns, that their knowledge of poetry is about up to the standard of a schoolboy, and their grammar somewhat below. Any one wishing to know how criticisms should not be written had better read the compilation—it would also be advisable to peruse the criticism which that journal ventured on its own responsibility. The reflection of the reader will be that if too much learning has made people mad, a want of it makes them idiots, and that whatever nonsense the poets may have written, it is infinitely more valuable than such sense. He will find that the whole interior press was in a state of eruption with epithets. And all because the madrigals of a McDonald, the epithalamiums of a Goodman, and the lively *chansonettes* which have from time to time rippled from the pens of a McCarthy or a McMuggins, were omitted from a volume which could scarcely have printed the names of all these sucking bards—let alone a list of their works. Enough stones were thrown at the editor to build his monument, and enough mud was showered upon one of the contributors—erroneously conjectured to be concerned in the compilation of the volume —to cement that monument together. In nature these notices were essentially alike, the only variation being in length; and here the palm must be awarded to one which had origin in the sage brush and might have been written by a *sage-femme* —for it was filled in with the minutest details of a profession which is not commonly canvassed in public. These bulletins being written, almost without exception, by men who do not know an iambus from an omnibus, or a pentameter from a potato, their value as poetic criticisms and the reason of the omission of the epics of the authors from the volume will be at once appreciated and understood.

The notices which we reproduce from critical journals of the East are in the main good. There is an affectation of *dilettanteism* about some of them, an assumption of patronizing superiority, which amuses rather than provokes, for it is not ill-natured. For this we imagine the editor of the book is in great degree responsible, since it is from his preface that they take their cue. It was scarcely necessary, we think, for him to appear hat in hand in the attitude of an apology for those whom he introduced before an excuse was asked of him for their appearance. And we imagine that there are a number of the contributors who would have refrained from appearing at all had they known that the voice of Bret the Baptist would be heard crying in the wilderness before them, in an attempt to make the path straight. Why did he not throw in a leavening lump or two of his own verse, and so save the necessity for a deprecating preface? It would have added materially to the success, as well as to the interest of the book.

The critic of the *Nation* naively confesses his surprise on finding some of the verses "sweet and tender, and at times *almost* original." He traces the "erotic nature" of some of the verse to "the fervor of California suns," which indicates that his knowledge of the peculiarities of our climate is neither extended enough nor sufficiently accurate to enable him to judge very discriminatively of what Mr. Bret calls "climatic influences." We scarcely think the gentleman would find himself very erotically inspired, if he were caught out on one of our July afternoons, a fog rolling in from the sea, no overcoat on, and one of the peculiar zephyrs which prevail at that season of the year tearing out his hair by the roots. And he does Bowman great injustice in supposing that he has never written better verses than the little couplets copied. Our word for it, that lyric of Frogtown is not "Bowman's Best." The most extended notice which the book receives is from the *Evening Post*, and if, as the *Morning Call* plausibly supposes and positively asserts, it be written by the editor, William Cullen Bryant—the *laudari a laudato viro* is not wanting in this instance. The most fair and generous notice comes from the *Times*. A reason for the lack of "local color" in the verse is found, not in climatic influences, but in the simple and very palpable fact that the writers were not born in California, but adopted it as their home after their habits of thought, feeling, and expression were fixed. The critic very sensibly assumes that a bullfinch brought out here, after having learned its notes at home, would probably pipe about the same as before, though the native quail has a different whistle from that of the Eastern bird. And he recognizes the fact that very many of the pieces have been floating upon the waves of ultramontane journalism for a year or two past, without credit to either the author or the paper in which they originally appeared. From the fact that these pieces have been taken at second-hand so gladly, we think we have ample grounds for venturing the assertion that they would still more gladly have been accepted as original contributions. And when these same journals, which have leaned upon our poets' arms in their weekly walks, turn around and pat them upon the head, and remark that they are glad to see how well they are learning to toddle, we feel like entering a very emphatic protest. There is an outspoken candor and sincerity in the *Times'* criticism which we like. Without any weak preludes, qualifying phrases, regrets, or invidious comparisons, it says of the little volume what every unprejudiced mind must acknowledge "few miscellaneous collections of poetry rise to a higher degree of merit." Going a step farther we maintain that the book contains a number of *poems*—not pieces of *verse*—which would find admittance to the most exigeant magazines, and very few that would be refused by any literary journal if contributed to it, as they have been to California journals, gratuitously. Poetry, unfortunately, is not paid for in this country —let us at least give our bards that praise which is their due, and which the verdict of the press of older states, quite as entitled to critical pretensions as our own, is not slow to accord them.

CALIFORNIAN, *January* 20, 1866.

CHAPTER XIX

Condensed Novels and the Lost Galleon

HARTE'S FIRST BOOK

BRET HARTE'S "Condensed Novels."—Carleton and Co., of New York, have just published in a small volume, the humorous travesties of a number of the best known English and American novelists, by Frank Bret Harte. The book also includes a selection from the author's admirable sketches, such as "The Venerable Impostor," "My Newfoundland Dog," etc. A considerable number of these pieces appeared in THE CALIFORNIAN, but they possess more than a local or ephemeral interest, and are well worthy of preservation in a permanent form. The New York *Tribune*, speaking of the travesties and sketches that compose the volume, says:

"They contain many effective hits at the mannerisms of certain celebrated writers, without the extravagance and forced attempts at wit which makes so many productions of the kind as vapid as an uncorked bottle of Congress water. Although written, as the author confesses, for an ephemeral purpose, they exhibit qualities which entitle them to preservation in a more permanent form, and will serve as authentic illustrations of a peculiar phase of American humor."

We shall avail ourselves of an early opportunity of speaking more at length of Mr. Harte's first serious attempt at authorship.

CALIFORNIAN, *November 2, 1867.*

MR. HARTE'S NEW BOOK*

The Sacramento *Union*, which enjoys a higher reputation for the accuracy of its reports of "Supreme Court decisions," the fullness and general excellence of its news department, and even for its editorial ability, than for the taste and discrimination of its literary criticism, speaks of these fine and exquisitely finished sketches as "of a coarse texture," the very last comment, one would imagine, that any judicious or appreciative critic would make upon anything, either in prose or verse, from the pen of Mr. Harte. It is charitable to assume that the "general utility editor" of the *Union*, upon whom the comparatively unimportant work of pronouncing judgment on literary performances, devolved in the brief intervals of leisure snatched from the weightier duties of clipping exchanges, and devising sensational headings for the despatches, was unable to devote any portion of his valuable time to the perusal of the book, and so derived his idea of the quality of its humor, from the quality of the wretched illustrations by which it is disfigured. The *Union's* largeness and liberality of spirit toward California writers, is no less strikingly exemplified in its notice of this book, than its rare literary discrimination. It disposes in *eleven* slovenly lines, of this first serious essay at authorship, of perhaps the most distinguished, and certainly the most graceful and finished writer on the coast, while in contrast to this boorish and niggard treatment, a New York daily paper, the *Evening Mail*, devotes over a column to it. The New York critic, differing *toto cœlo* with the "reviewer" of the *Union*, declares that the humor of Mr. Harte is characterized by "a delicacy and good taste which makes a pleasant contrast with the usual broad and coarse character of burlesque imitations," adding that the author is evidently "a gentleman, as well as a humorist, and never drops one role for the other." Without attempting at pres-

---

* "Condensed Novels and Other Papers," by F. Bret Harte. New York: G. W. Carleton & Co. San Francisco: A. Roman & Co.

ent any formal criticism of Mr. Harte's book, we will content ourselves with a few extracts, from which our readers may form their own estimate of its merits. In the following, few will have any difficulty in recognizing the salient characteristics of Charles Lever:

In an instant I was engaged with an entire squadron of cavalry who endeavored to surround me. Cutting my way through them, I advanced boldly upon a battery, and sabred the gunners before they could bring their pieces to bear. Looking around, I saw that I had in fact penetrated the French center. Before I was well aware of the locality, I was hailed by a sharp voice in French:

"Come here, sir!"

I obeyed, and advanced to the side of a little man in a cocked hat.

"Has Grouchy come?"

"Not yet, sire," I replied—for it was the Emperor.

"Ha!" he said suddenly, bending his piercing eyes on my uniform—"a prisoner?"

"No, sire," I said, proudly.

"A spy?"

I placed my hand upon my sword, but a gesture from the Emperor made me forbear.

"You are a brave man," he said.

I took my snuff box from my pocket, and taking a pinch, replied by handing it, with a bow, to the Emperor.

His quick eye caught the cypher on the lid.

"What! a D'Euville? Ha! this accounts for the purity of your accent. Any relation to Roderick D'Euville?"

"My father, sire."

"He was my schoolfellow at the Ecole Politechnique. Embrace me!" and the Emperor fell upon my neck in the presence of his entire staff. Then recovering himself, he gently placed in my hand his own magnificent snuffbox in exchange for mine, and hanging upon my breast the cross of the Legion of Honor which he took from his own, he bade one of his Marshalls conduct me back to my regiment.

I was so intoxicated with the honor of which I had been the recipient, that on reaching our lines I uttered a shout of joy and put spurs to my horse. The intelligent animal seemed to sympathize with my feelings, and fairly flew over the ground. On a rising eminence a few yards before me stood a gray-haired officer, surrounded by his staff. I don't know what possessed me, but putting spurs to my horse, I rode at him boldly, and with one bound cleared him, horse and all. A shout of indignation arose from the assembled staff. I wheeled suddenly, with the intention of apologizing, but my mare misunderstood me, and again dashing forward, once more vaulted over the head of the officer, this time unfortunately uncovering him by a vicious kick of her hoof. "Seize him!" roared the entire army. I was seized. As the soldiers led me away, I asked the name of the gray haired officer. "That—, why, that's the *Duke of Wellington!*"

I fainted.

Some of the minor traits and mannerisms of the author of "Jane Eyrie" are thus happily hit off:

The wind howled dismally without, and the rain beat furiously against the windows. I crept toward him and seated myself on a low stool beside his chair.

Presently he turned without seeing me and placed his foot absently in my lap. I affected not to notice it. But he started and looked down.

"You here yet—Carrothead? Ah, I forgot. Do you speak French!"

"*Oui, Monsieur.*"

"*Taisez-vous!*" he said sharply, with singular purity of accent. I complied. The wind moaned fearfully in the chimney, and the light burned dim. I shuddered in spite of myself. "Ah, you tremble, girl!"

"It is a fearful night."

"Fearful! Call you this fearful, ha! ha! ha? Look! you wretched little atom, look!" and he dashed forward, and leaping out of the window, stood like a statue in the pelting storm. He did not stay long, but in a few minutes returned by the way of the hall chimney. I saw from the way that he wiped his feet on my dress that he had again forgotten my presence.

"You are a governess. What can you teach?" he asked suddenly and fiercely thrusting his face in mine.

"Manners!" I replied calmly.

"Ha! teach *me*."

"You mistake yourself," I said, adjusting my mittens. "Your manners require not the artificial restraint of society. You are radically polite; this impetuosity and ferociousness is simply the sincerity which is the basis of a proper deportment. Your instincts are moral; your better nature, I see, is religious. As St. Paul justly remarks—see chap. 6, 8, 9 and 10—"

He seized a heavy candlestick, and threw it at me. I dodged it submissively, but firmly.

"Excuse me," he remarked, as the under jaw relaxed. "Excuse me, Miss Mix; but I can't stand St. Paul! Enough—you are engaged."

The treatment of the "Sword and Gown" style is excellent. Here is a piece of it:

Suddenly came a dull, crashing sound from the school-room. At the ominous interruption I shuddered involuntarily, and called to Smithsye:

"What's up, Smithums?"

"Guy's cleaning out the fourth form," he replied.

At the same moment George de Coverly passed me, holding his nose, from whence the bright Norman blood streamed redly. To him the plebian Smithsye laughingly cried:

"Cully! how's his nibs?"

I pushed the door of the school-room open. There are some spectacles which a man never forgets. The burning of Troy

probably seemed a large sized conflagration to the pious
Æneas, and made an impression on him which he carried
away with the feeble Anchises.

In the center of the room, lightly brandishing the pistol-
rod of a steam engine, stood Guy Heavystone alone. I say
alone, for the pile of small boys on the floor could hardly be
called company.

I will try and sketch him for the reader. Guy Heavystone
was then only fifteen. His broad, deep chest, his sinewy and
quivering flank, his straight bastern showed him to be a thor-
ough-bred. Perhaps he was a trifle heavy in the fetlock but he
held his head haughtily erect. His eyes were glittering but
pitiless. There was a sternness about the lower part of his
face—the old Heavystone look—a sternness, heightened,
perhaps, by the snaffle-bit which, in one of his strange freaks,
he wore in his mouth to curb his occasional ferocity.

Perhaps, however, the best burlesques, are those of Victor
Hugo, and the author of Guy Livingstone. Cooper's high
idealization of the Indian character, too, offered a capital
opening for Mr. Harte's peculiar vein of humor, which he has
not failed to take advantage of. In addition to the "Condensed Novels," the volume contains a number of papers
and sketches contributed to various periodicals, among
others, the *Atlantic Monthly*. From one of these, entitled
"Sidewalkings," we quote the following:

Speaking of eyes, you can generally settle the average
gentility and good breeding of the people you meet in the
street by the manner in which they return or evade your
glance. "A gentleman," as the Autocrat has wisely said, is
always "calm-eyed." There is just enough abstraction in his
look to denote his individual power and the capacity for self-
contemplation, while he is, nevertheless, quietly and unob-
trusively observant. He does not seek, neither does he evade,
your observation. Snobs and prigs do the first; bashful and
mean people do the second. There are some men who, on
meeting your eye, immediately assume an expression quite

different from the one which they previously wore, which, whether an improvement or not, suggests a disagreeable self-consciousness. Perhaps they fancy they are betraying something. There are others who return your look with unnecessary defiance, which suggests a like concealment. The symptoms of the eye are generally borne out in the figure. A man is very apt to betray his character by the manner in which he appropriates his part of the sidewalk. The man who resolutely keeps the middle of the pavement, and deliberately brushes against you, you may be certain would take the last piece of pie at the hotel table, and empty the cream jug on its way to your cup. The man who slides by you, keeping close to the horses, and selecting the easiest planks, manages to slip through life in some such way, and to evade its sternest duties. The awkward man, who gets in your way, and throws you back upon the man behind you, and so manages to derange the harmonious procession of a whole block, is very apt to do the same thing in political and social economy.

This volume fully establishes Mr. Harte's title to an honorable rank among the best class of American humorists; not among those whose humor smacks largely of buffoonery, and relies chiefly for its effect upon verbal extravagancies and tricks of phraseology, but with such writers as Holmes, Donald G. Mitchell, and William Henry Curtis, of the last of whom he frequently reminds us. His points are delicately made, in the spirit of a true artist, and his satire often has the fine edge of Thackeray's, not without something of its semicynical quality. The critic of the *Bulletin* does the author no more than simple justice, when he says of these sketches: "So fine is the fancy, so subtle the wit, that they almost escape us before we have fully tasted and enjoyed them. And it is because of the fineness of the quality, and not from poverty of idea, that he sometimes fails to satisfy the average popular want. Were his standard less high and his taste less severe, he would doubtless prove a greater favorite with the million; but a writer of such sterling merit can afford to bide his time, and work rather for permanent fame than ephemeral applause."

To speak of the humor manifested in the book as "of a somewhat coarse texture," is simply to prove that the critic who employs such language is as incompetent to pass upon literary performances of the character of these papers, as a confirmed drunkard whose palate has been demoralized by bad whisky, would be to judge of the quality of a fine wine.

CALIFORNIAN, *November* 16, 1867.

MR. HARTE CRITICISED

The *Territorial Enterprise* publishes the following notice of Mr. Harte's "Condensed Novels," in which the very grave charge is made against the author—and we think with perfect justice—that "his tastes fetter him to the classical models of the language." The same damaging objection of undue respect for "classical models," was recently made by the Nevada critic against Mr. Stoddard's poems:

Without time to thoroughly examine the contents of this volume, we shall speak of it and its author in general terms, reflecting the impressions we have derived from the perusal of numerous articles contributed by him to the journals of this coast. Mr. Harte is the most finished and pleasing writer California has yet produced. His taste is exquisite, his diction faultless. His perception of the humorous is more delicate than that of a dozen or so professed humorists of California, in addition to which he displays what no other living writer of his State has exhibited—genuine wit. Yet with all these rare qualities he has failed to accomplish any marked success in letters, and appears as likely hereafter to fail in any signal achievement in literature. His tastes fetter him to the classical models of the language. He seems to think it incumbent upon him to issue his productions on the collateral security of some acknowledged author. This assimilation, or over-cautiousness—or whatever it may be—on the part of Mr. Harte, has led to the preferment of charges of plagiarism against him by members of the opposition press; but all the proofs they have ever adduced have been far-fetched and un-substantial. The mistake they made was in endeavoring to convict him of felony, when the offense—if that may be called an offense which injures nobody and delights every one —was that of imitation. Imitating the cut of another man's coat, and appropriating said garment itself, are two different things. Thus, we venture to say, Mr. Harte has never abso-lutely appropriated any author's vestment, though he may have shaped his material to the pattern of many an admired mantle. The "Condensed Novels" of Mr. Harte are ac-knowledged and obvious types of all his writings. Whether credited or not, they are all copies—more or less free in draw-ing and tone—from approved originals. But if—as maybe the case—the gentleman's productions thus far are the purposed results of a severe schooling in art—if, with commendable zeal, he has devoted his youthful energies to the patient study of the masters—he has been eminently successful, and in good time will bring rare skill to the execution of his original conceptions. The present volume is a collection of sketches published during the past five years, principally in California journals. It is one of the most entertaining works in the range of light literature, and possesses peculiar interest to the readers of this coast, being of a local character.

CALIFORNIAN, *November* 23, 1867.

"THE LOST GALLEON"

The Lost Galleon, and Other Tales, is the title of a little volume of verse by Frank Bret Harte, just published by the author, and printed by Towne & Bacon. As a specimen of book-making in all its mechanical departments it is alto-gether admirable, and so superior to many Californian pro-

ductions that are brought out at the East, that we hope Mr.
Harte will forward a copy to Carleton & Co., who published
his "Condensed Novels," in order to afford those gentlemen
an opportunity of comparing the two. Besides "The Lost
Galleon," "John Burns of Gettysburg," "The Tale of a
Pony," "The Ballad of the Emeu," "North Beach," "To
the Pliocene Skull," the book contains a considerable number
of pieces not inferior to these, though less familiar to the
reading public of California. The author introduces his volume with the following highly characteristic verses:

> Behind the footlights hangs the rusty baize;
> A trifle shabby in the upturned blaze
> Of flaring gas, and curious eyes that gaze.
>
> The stage, methinks, perhaps is none too wide;
> And hardly fit for royal Richard's stride,
> Or Falstaff's bulk, or Denmark's youthful pride.
>
> Ah well! no passion walks its humble boards—
> O'er it no king nor valiant Hector lords—
> The simplest skill is all its space affords—
>
> The song and jest, the dance and trifling play—
> The local hit at follies of the day—
> The trick to pass an idle hour away—
>
> For these, no trumpets that announce the Moor—
> No blast that makes the hero's welcome sure—
> A single fiddle in the overture!

Although there are several poems in the book that we have
been accustomed to rank as among the best of their class, by
any American writer, the impression produced by them upon
a re-reading in the present collected form, is not less favorable. One of the author's most powerful literary instincts
seems to be a horror of the exaggerated, the unreal, and false
in sentiment and passion. This instinct, while it guards a
writer against the danger of doing anything that can be made
to appear absurd, sometimes exercises an injurious effect by
too closely restricting the natural impulses of genius. There

are some notable literary performances which the world is the better for, and could not willingly spare, which could not have been produced by men of a cautious and critical turn of mind, and possessed of a quick and delicate perception of the ludicrous or unheroic aspects of things. We have said that Mr. Harte's introductory verses are "highly characteristic," and when we add that we do not exactly like them, might be understood as meaning that we do not admire the author's writings. This, however, is not our meaning, since "Before the Curtain" is marked by *the only* quality in Mr. Harte's productions that affects us disagreeably, a certain something that it would be inexact to call an affectation of self-disparagement, but which we can at present find no other name for. He offers us a volume of poems, excellent in their kind, nearly perfect as literary compositions, and calculated to charm the taste of all cultivated readers. And yet, he cannot permit us to sit down to enjoyment of the feast, without first entering a formal protest against being supposed to labor under the illusion that he has done anything worth speaking of, and solemnly cautioning his readers against doing him such an injustice by imagining that *he* attaches any value to such literary trifles. "Before the Curtain" is not, however, the key note to the volume. It contains several poems that evince no trace of critical consciousness, and many that are exquisite for delicacy and beauty. No such elegant volume has ever been printed in California, and we hope that it may find a place on every center table in the State.

CALIFORNIAN, *December* 21, 1867.

CHAPTER XX

Editorial Changes

ʙᴇᴛ Hᴀʀᴛᴇ did his first work as an editor on Tʜᴇ Cᴀʟɪғᴏʀɴɪᴀɴ. He was editor for a brief period on two different occasions. This experience was undoubtedly very valuable to him when he later became editor of the Overland Monthly.—Eᴅɪᴛᴏʀ.

"Tʜᴇ Cᴀʟɪғᴏʀɴɪᴀɴ, *September* 10, 1864.

"In the change of a name at the head of this paper, and of a personal influence in its columns, the undersigned trusts will hereafter be found the only essential alteration in that general character and design which have made it acceptable to its readers."

F. B. Hᴀʀᴛᴇ.

'Tʜᴇ Cᴀʟɪғᴏʀɴɪᴀɴ," *November* 26, 1864.

The present number (November 26, 1864) of Tʜᴇ Cᴀʟɪғᴏʀɴɪᴀɴ witnesses a change in the proprietorship and editorial control. For the future it will be published by "Tʜᴇ Cᴀʟɪғᴏʀɴɪᴀɴ Pʀɪɴᴛɪɴɢ ᴀɴᴅ Pᴜʙʟɪsʜɪɴɢ Cᴏᴍᴘᴀɴʏ." Frank Bret Harte retires from the editorial chair, and C. H. Webb re-assumes the position which he occupied at the foundation of the paper.

"Tʜᴇ Cᴀʟɪғᴏʀɴɪᴀɴ," *December* 9, 1865.

Francis Bret Harte becomes editor.

"Tʜᴇ Cᴀʟɪғᴏʀɴɪᴀɴ," *December* 30, 1865.

With the close of this year Francis Bret Harte retires from Tʜᴇ Cᴀʟɪғᴏʀɴɪᴀɴ.

Sketches of the Sixties

MARK TWAIN

MONTGOMERY STREET AT CALIFORNIA STREET, SAN FRANCISCO
IN THE SIXTIES

THE office of THE CALIFORNIAN, the literary journal for which
Bret Harte and Mark Twain were writing, was in this block (the
water-wagon is standing immediately in front of the publication office!) during the brief period when Harte was editor for
the first time. The American Trust Bank now stands on this site.
On the corner diagonally across the street will be seen the building erected in 1852 and occupied by Wells Fargo & Company for
more than a quarter of a century. This building was constructed of stone blocks cut in China and built by Chinese workmen
brought over especially for the purpose. It was one of the few
structures in the downtown section not destroyed by the fire
of 1906. The new Financial Center building now
occupies this location.

CHAPTER I

𝕬 𝕹otable Conundrum

T HE FAIR continues, just the same. It is a nice place to hunt for people in. I have hunted for a friend there for as much as two hours of an evening, and at the end of that time found the hunting just as good as it was when I commenced.

If the projectors of this noble Fair never receive a dollar or even a kindly word of thanks for the labor of their hands, the sweat of their brows and the wear and tear of brain it has cost them to plan their work and perfect it, a consciousness of the incalculable good they have conferred upon the community must still give them a placid satisfaction more precious than money or sounding compliments. They have been the means of bringing many a pair of loving hearts together that could not get together anywhere else on account of parents and other obstructions. When you see a young lady standing by the sanitary scarecrow which mutely appeals to the public for quarters and swallows them, you may know by the expectant look upon her face that a young man is going to happen along there presently; and, if you have my luck, you will notice by that look still remaining upon her face that you are not the young man she is expecting. They court a good deal at the Fair, and the young fellows are always exchanging notes with the girls. For this purpose the business cards scattered about the place are found very convenient. I picked up one last night which was printed on both sides, but had been interlined in pencil, by somebody's Arabella, until one could not read it without feeling dizzy. It ran about in this wise—though the interlineations were not in parentheses in the original:

"John Smith, (My Dearest and Sweetest:) Soap Boiler and Candle Factor; (If you love me, if you love) Bar Soap, Castile Soap and Soft Soap, peculiarly suitable for (your Arabella, fly to the) Pacific coast, because of its non-liability to be affected by the climate. Those who may have kitchen refuse to sell, can leave orders, and our soap-fat carts will visit the (Art Gallery. I will be in front of the big mirror in an hour from now, and will go with you to the) corner designated. For the very best Soap and Candles the market affords, apply at the (Academy of Music. And from there, O joy! how my heart thrills with rapture at the prospect! with souls surcharged with bliss, we will wander forth to the) Soap Factory, or to the office, which is located on the (moon-lit beach,) corner of Jackson street, near the milk ranch. (From Arabella, who sends kisses to her darling) JOHN SMITH, Pioneer Soap Boiler and Candle Factor."

Sweethearts usually treasure up these little affectionate billets, and that this one was lost in the Pavilion, seemed proof to me that its contents were rather distracting to the mind of the young man who received it. He never would have lost it if he had not felt unsettled about something. I think it is likely he got mixed, so to speak, as to whether he was the lucky party, or whether it was the soap-boiler. However, I have possession of her extraordinary document now, and this is to inform Arabella that, in the hope that I may answer for the other young man, and do to fill a void or so in her aching heart, I am drifting about, in an unsettled way, on the lookout for her—sometimes on the Pacific Coast, sometimes at the Art Gallery, sometimes at the soap factory, and occasionally at the moonlit beach and the milk ranch. If she happen to visit either of those places shortly, and will have the goodness to wait a little while, she can calculate on my drifting around in the course of an hour or so.

I cannot say that all visitors to the Fair go there to make love, though I have my suspicions that a good many of them do. Numbers go there to look at the machinery and misunderstand it, and still greater numbers, perhaps, go to criticise the pictures. There is a handsome portrait in the Art Gallery of a pensive young girl. Last night it fell under the critical eye of a connoisseur from Arkansas. She examined it in silence for many minutes, and then she blew her nose calmly, and, says she, "I like it—it is so sad and thinkful."

Somebody knocked Weller's bust down from its shelf at the Fair, the other night, and destroyed it. It was wrong to do it, but it gave rise to a very able pun by a young person who has had much experience in such things, and was only indifferently proud of it. He said it was Weller enough when it was a bust, but just the reverse when it was busted. Explanation: He meant that it looked like Weller in the first place, but it did not after it was smashed to pieces. He also meant that it was well enough to leave it alone and not destroy it. The Author of this fine joke is among us yet, and I can bring him around if you would like to look at him. One would expect him to be haughty and ostentatious, but you would be surprised to see how simple and unpretending he is and how willing to take a drink.

But I have been playing the noble game of "Muggins." In that game, if you make a mistake of any kind, however trivial it may be, you are pronounced a muggins by the whole company, with great unanimity and enthusiasm. If you play the right card in the wrong place, you are a muggins; no matter how you play, in nine cases out of ten you are a muggins. They inform you of it with a shout which has no expression in it of regret. I have played this fine game all the evening, and although I knew little about it at first, I got to be quite a muggins at last. I played it very successfully on a policeman as I went home. I had forgotten my night-key and was climbing in at the window. When he clapped his hand on my shoulder, I smiled upon him and, says I, "Muggins!" with much vivacity. Says he, "How so?" and I said, "Because I live here, and you play the wrong card when you arrest me for entering my own house." I thought it was rather neat. But then there was nobody at home to identify me, and I had to go all the way to the station-house with him and give bail to appear and answer to a charge of burglary. As I turned to depart says he "Muggins!" I thought that was rather neat also.

But the conundrum I have alluded to in the heading of this article, was the best thing of the kind that has ever fallen under my notice. It was projected by a young man who has hardly any education at all, and whose opportunities have been very meagre, even from his childhood up. It was this: "Why was Napoleon when he crossed the Alps, like the Sanitary cheese at the Mechanics' Fair?"

It was very good for a young man just starting in life; don't you think so? He has gone away now to Sacramento. Probably we shall never see him more. He did not state what the answer was.   MARK TWAIN.

CALIFORNIAN, *October* 1, 1864.

CHAPTER II

Concerning the Answer to that Conundrum

I WENT out, several days ago, to see the whale—I speak in the singular number, because there was only one whale on the beach at that time. The day was excessively warm, and my comrade was an invalid; consequently we travelled slowly, and conversed about distressing diseases and such other matters as I thought would be likely to interest a sick man and make him feel cheerful. Instead of commenting on the mild scenery we found on the route, we spoke of the ravages of the cholera in the happy days of our boyhood; instead of talking about the warm weather, we revelled in bilious fever reminiscences; instead of boasting of the extraordinary swiftness of our horse, as most persons similarly situated would have done, we chatted gaily of consumption; and when we caught a glimpse of long white lines of waves rolling in silently upon the distant shore, our hearts were gladdened and our stomachs turned by fond memories of sea-sickness. It was a nice comfortable journey, and I could not have enjoyed it more if I had been sick myself.

When we got to the Cliff House we were disappointed. I had always heard there was such a grand view to be seen there of the majestic ocean, with its white billows stretching far away until it met and mingled with the bending sky; with here and there a stately ship upon its surface, ploughing through plains of sunshine and deserts of shadow cast from the clouds above; and, near at hand, piles of picturesque rocks, splashed with angry surf and garrisoned by drunken, sprawling sea-lions and elegant, long-legged pelicans.

It was a bitter disappointment. There was nothing in sight but an ordinary counter, and behind it a long row of bottles with Old Bourbon, and Old Rye, and Old Tom, and the old, old story of man's falter and woman's fall, in them. Nothing in the world to be seen but these things. We staid there an hour and a half, and took observations from different points of view, but the general result was the same—nothing but bottles and a bar. They keep a field-glass there, for the accommodation of those who wish to see the sights, and we looked at the bottles through that, but it did not help the matter any to speak of; we turned it end for end, but instead of increasing the view it diminished it. If it had not been fashionable, I would not have engaged in this trivial amusement; I say trivial, because, notwithstanding they said everybody used the glass, I still consider it trivial amusement, and very undignified, to sit staring at a row of gin-bottles through an opera-glass. Finally, we tried a common glass tumbler, and found that it answered just as well, on account of the close proximity of the scenery, and did not seem quite so stupid. We continued to use it, and the more we got accustomed to it, the better we liked it. Although tame enough at first, the effects eventually became really extraordinary. The single row of bottles doubled, and then trebled itself, and finally became a sort of dissolving view of inconceivable beauty and confusion. When Johnny first looked through the tumbler, he said: "It is rather a splendid display, isn't it?" and an hour afterwards he said: "Thas so—'s a sp-(ic!)-splennid 'splay!" and set his glass down with sufficient decision to break it.

We went out, then, and saw a sign marked "CHICKEN SHOOTING," and we sat down and waited a long time, but finally we got weary and discouraged, and my comrade said that perhaps it was no use—may be the chicken was not going to shoot that day. We did not mind the disappointment so much, but the hiccups were so distressing. I am subject to them when I go abroad.

We left the hotel, then, and drove along the level beach, drowsily admiring the terraced surf, and listening to the tidings it was bringing from other lands in the mysterious language of its ceaseless roar, until we hove in sight of the stranded whale. We thought it was a cliff, an isolated hill, an island—anything but a fish, capable of being cut up and stowed away in a ship. Its proportions were magnified a thousand-fold beyond any conception we had previously formed of them. We felt that we could not complain of a disappointment in regard to the whale, at any rate. But we were not prepared to see a magnified mastodon, also; yet there seemed to be one towering high above the beach not far f om the whale. We drove a hundred yards further—it was nothing but a horse.

Then the light of inspiration dawned upon me, and I knew what I would do if I kept the hotel, and the whale belonged to me. I would not permit any one to approach nearer than six or eight hundred yards to the show, because at that distance the light mists, or the peculiar atmosphere, or something, exaggerates it into a monster of colossal size. It grows smaller as you go towards it. When we got pretty close to it, the island shrunk into a fish—a very large one for a sardine, it is true, but a very small one for a whale—and the mastodon dwindled down to a Cayuse pony. Distance had been lending immensity to the view. We were disappointed again somewhat; but see how things are regulated! The very source of our disappointment was a blessing to us: As it was, there was just as much smell as two of us could stand; and if the fish had been larger there would have been more, wouldn't there? and where could we have got assistance on that lonely beach to help us smell it? Ah! it was the great law of compensation—the great law that regulates Nature's heedless agents, and sees that when they make a mistake, they shall at the self-same moment prevent that mistake from working evil consequences. Behold, the same gust of wind that blows a lady's dress aside, and exposes her ankle, fills your eyes so full of sand that you can't see it. Marvellous are the works of Nature!

The whale was not a long one, physically speaking—say thirty-five feet—but he smelt much longer; he smelt as much as a mile and a half longer, I should say, for we traveled about that distance beyond him before we ceased to detect his fragrance in the atmosphere. My comrade said he did not admire to smell a whale; and I adopt his sentiments while I scorn his language. A whale does not smell like magnolia, nor yet like heliotrope or "Balm of a Thousand Flowers;" I do now know, but I should judge that it smells more like a thousand pole-cats.

With these few remarks I will now proceed to unfold a conundrum which I consider one of the finest that has ever emanated from the human mind. My invalid comrade produced it while we were driving along slowly in the open country this side of the Ocean House. I think it was just where we crossed the aqueduct of the Spring Valley Water Company, though I will not be certain; it might have been a little to the east of it, or maybe a little to the west, but at any rate it was in the immediate vicinity of it. I remember the time, though, very distinctly, for I was looking at my watch at the moment he commenced speaking, and it was a quarter of a minute after 3 o'clock—I made a memorandum of it afterward in my note-book which I will show you if you will remind me of it when I visit the CALIFORNIAN office. The sun was shining very brightly, but a light breeze was blowing from the sea, which rendered the weather pleasanter than it had been for several hours previously, and as it blew the dust in the same direction in which we were traveling, we experienced no inconvenience from it, although, as a general thing, I do not enjoy dust. It was under these circumstances that my invalid comrade, young John William Skae, who is in the quartz-milling business in Virginia City, now, but was born in the State of Pennsylvania, where his parents, and in fact most of his relatives, still reside, except one of his brothers,

who is in the army, and his aunt, who married a minister of
the gospel and is living out West, sometimes having an improving season in the vineyard and sometimes chased around
considerable by the bushwhackers, who cannot abide preachers, and who stir them up impartially, just the same as they
do those who have not yet got religion; and also except his
first cousin, James Peterson, who is a skirmisher and is with
the parson—he goes through the camp-meetings and skir-
mishes for raw converts, whom he brings to the front and
puts them in the corral, or the mourner's bench, as they call
it in that section, so that the parson can exhort them more
handy—it was under these circumstances, as I was saying,
that young Skae, who had been ruminating in dead silence
for a long time, turned toward me with an unwholesome glare
in his eye, at a quarter of a minute after 3 o'clock, while we
were in the vicinity of the aqueduct of the Spring Valley
Water Company, and notwithstanding the light breeze that
was blowing and the filmy dust that was drifting about us,
says he: "Why is a whale like a certain bird which has blue
feathers and is mostly found in the West, where he is considered a good bird though not remarkable? It is, because he is
the Kingfisher—(the king fish, sir.)"

There was no house near by, except an old shed that had
been used by some workmen, but I took him to that and did
what I could for him; his whole nervous system seemed pros-
trated; he only raised his head once, and asked in a feeble
voice, but with an expression of ineffable satisfaction in it—
"How's that?" I knew he did not want medicine—if anything could save him, it would be rest and quiet. Therefore, I
removed the horses to a distance, and then went down the
road, and by representing the case fairly and openly to all
passengers, I got them to drive by him slowly so that they
would make no noise to excite him. My efforts were successful; his pulse was at two hundred and ninety when I put him
in the shed, and only forty-two when I took him out.

Now I thought that conundrum would have done honor to

the finest mind among us, and I think it especially good for an invalid from Pennsylvania. How does it strike you? It is circumscribed in its action, though, and is applicable only to men; you could not say "Because it is the king fish, madam," without marring the effect of the joke by rendering the point in a manner obscure.

Some friends of mine of great powers and high intellectual culture, and who naturally take an interest in conundrums, besought me to procure the answer to that one about Napoleon and the Sanitary cheese, and publish it. I have written to the Author of it, and he informs me that he and his mother, who is a woman of extraordinary sagacity and a profound thinker, are cyphering at it night and day, and they confidently expect to have the answer ready in time for your next week's issue. From what I can understand, they are making very encouraging progress; they have already found out why Napoleon was like the cheese, but thus far they have not been able to ascertain in what respect the cheese resembles Napoleon.   MARK TWAIN.

CALIFORNIAN, *October* 8, 1864.

CHAPTER III

𝔖till 𝔍urther 𝔠oncerning that 𝔠onundrum

IN ACCORDANCE with your desire, I went to the Academy of Music on Monday evening, to take notes and prepare myself to write a careful critique upon the opera of the *Crown Diamonds*. That you considered me able to acquit myself creditably in this exalted sphere of literary labor, was gratifying to me, and I should even have felt flattered by it had I not known that I was so competent to perform the task well, that to set it for me could not be regarded as a flattering concession, but, on the contrary, only a just and deserved recognition of merit.

Now, to throw disguise aside and speak openly, I have long yearned for an opportunity to write an operatic diagnostical and analytical dissertation for you. I feel the importance of carefully-digested newspaper criticism in matters of this kind —for I am aware that by it the dramatic and musical tastes of a community are moulded, cultivated and irrevocably fixed—that by it these tastes are vitiated and debased, or elevated and ennobled, according to the refinement or vulgarity, and the competency or incompetency of the writers to whom this department of the public training is entrusted. If you would see around you a people who are filled with the keenest appreciation of perfection in musical execution and dramatic delineation, and painfully sensitive to the slightest departures from the true standard of art in these things, you must employ upon your newspapers critics capable of discriminating between merit and demerit, and alike fearless in praising the

one and condemning the other. Such a person—although it
may be in some degree immodest in me to say so—I claim to
be. You will not be surprised, then, to know that I read your
boshy criticisms on the opera with the most exquisite anguish
—and not only yours, but those which I find in every paper in
San Francisco.

You do nothing but sing one everlasting song of praise;
when an artist, by diligence and talent, makes an effort of
transcendent excellence, behold, instead of receiving marked
and cordial attention, both artist and effort sink from sight,
and are lost in the general slough of slimy praise in which it
is your pleasure to cause the whole company, good, bad and
indifferent, to wallow once a week. With this brief but very
liberal and hearty expression of sentiment, I will drop the
subject and leave you alone for the present, for it behooves
me now to set you a model in criticism.

The opera of the *Crown Diamonds* was put upon the stage
in creditable shape on Monday evening, although I noticed
that the curtains of the "Queen of Portugal's" drawing-room
were not as gorgeous as they might have been, and that the
furniture had a second-hand air about it, of having seen service in the preceding reign. The acting and the vocalization,
however, were, in the main, good. I was particularly charmed
by the able manner in which Signor Bellindo Alphonso
Cellini, the accomplished basso-relievo furniture-scout and
sofa-shifter, performed his part. I have before observed that
this rising young artist gave evidence of the rarest genius in
his peculiar department of operatic business, and have been
annoyed at noticing with what studied care a venomous and
profligate press have suppressed his name and suffered his
sublimest efforts to pass unnoticed and unglorified. Shame
upon such grovelling envy and malice! But, with all your
neglect, you have failed to crush the spirit of the gifted furniture-scout, or seduce from him the affectionate encourage-
ment and appreciation of the people. The moment he stepped
upon the stage on Monday evening, to carry out the bandit

chieftain's valise, the upper circles, with one accord, shouted, "Supe! supe!" and greeted him with warm and generous applause. It was a princely triumph for Bellindo; he told me afterwards it was the proudest moment of his life.

I watched Alphonso during the entire performance and was never so well pleased with him before, although I have admired him from the first. In the second act, when the eyes of the whole audience were upon him—when his every movement was the subject of anxiety and suspense—when everything depended upon his nerve and self-possession, and the slightest symptom of hesitation or lack of confidence would have been fatal—he stood erect in front of the cave, looking calmly and unflinchingly down upon the camp-stool for several moments, as one who has made up his mind to do his great work or perish in the attempt, and then seized it and bore it in triumph to the foot-lights! It was a sublime spectacle. There was not a dry eye in the house. In that moment, not even the most envious and uncharitable among the noble youth's detractors would have had the hardihood to say he was not endowed with a lofty genius.

Again, in the scene where the Prime Minister's nephew is imploring the female bandit to fly to the carriage and escape impending wrath, and when dismay and confusion ruled the hour, how quiet, how unmoved, how grandly indifferent was Bellindo in the midst of it all!—what solidity of expression lay upon his countenance! While all save himself were unnerved by despair, he serenely put forth his finger and mashed to a shapeless pulp a mosquito that loitered upon the wall, yet betrayed no sign of agitation the while. Was there nothing in this lofty contempt for the dangers which surrounded him that marked the actor destined hereafter to imperishable renown?

Possibly upon that occasion when it was necessary for Alphonso to remove two chairs and a table during the shifting of the scenes, he performed his part with undue precipitation; with the table upside down upon his head, and grasping the corners with hands burdened with the chairs, he appeared to some extent undignified when he galloped across the stage. Generally his conception of his part is excellent, but in this case I am satisfied he threw into it an enthusiasm not required and also not warranted by the circumstances. I think that careful study and reflection will convince him that I am right, and that the author of the opera intended that in this particular instance the furniture should be carried out with impressive solemnity. That he had this in view is evidenced by the slow and stately measure of the music played by the orchestra at that juncture.

But the crowning glory of Cellini's performance that evening was the placing of a chair for the Queen of Portugal to sit down in after she had become fatigued by earnestly and elaborately abusing the Prime Minister for losing the Crown Diamonds. He did not grab the chair by the hind leg and shove it awkwardly at her Majesty; he did not seize it by the seat and thrust it ungracefully toward her; he did not handle it as though he was undecided about the strict line of his duty or ignorant of the proper manner of performing it. He did none of these things. With a coolness and confidence that evinced the most perfect conception and the most consummate knowledge of his part, he came gently forward and laid hold of that chair from behind, set it in its proper place with a movement replete with grace, and then leaned upon the back of it, resting his chin upon his hand, and in this position smiled a smile of transfigured sweetness upon the audience over the Queen of Portugal's head. There shone the inspired actor! and the people saw and acknowledged him; they waited respectfully for Miss Richings to finish her song, and then with one impulse they poured forth upon him a sweeping tempest of applause.

At the end of the piece the idolized furniture-scout and sofa-skirmisher was called before the curtain by an enthusiastic shouting and clapping of hands, but he was thrust aside, as usual, and other artists, (who chose to consider the compliment as intended for themselves), swept bowing and smirking along the footlights and received it. I swelled with indignation, but I summoned my fortitude and resisted the pressure successfully. I am still intact.

Take it altogether, the *Crown Diamonds* was really a creditable performance. I feel that I would not be doing my whole duty if I closed this critique without speaking of Miss Caroline Richings, Miss Jenny Kempton, Mr. Hill, Mr. Seguin and Mr. Peakes, all of whom did fair justice to their several parts, and deserve a passing notice. With study, perseverance and attention, I have no doubt these vocalists will in time achieve a gratifying success in their profession.

I believe I have nothing further to say. I will call around, to-morrow, after you have had time to read, digest and pass your judgment upon my criticism, and, if agreeable, I will hire out to you for some years in that line.

MARK TWAIN.

P. S.—No answer to that conundrum this week. On account of over-exertion on it the old woman has got to having fits here lately. However, it will be forthcoming yet, when she runs out of them, if she don't die in the meantime, and I trust she will not. We may as well prepare ourselves for the worst, though, for it is not to be disguised that they are shaking her up mighty lively.

CALIFORNIAN, *October 15, 1864.*

CHAPTER IV

Whereas, Love's Bakery

L OVE'S BAKERY! I am satisfied I have found
the place now that I have been looking for all
this time. I cannot describe to you the sensa-
sation of mingled astonishment, gladness,
hope, doubt, anxiety, and balmy, blissful
emotion that suffused my being and quivered
in a succession of streaky thrills down my backbone, as I
stood on the corner of Third and Minna streets, last Tuesday,
and stared, spell-bound, at those extraordinary words,
painted in large, plain letters on a neighboring window-cur-
tain—"LOVE'S BAKERY." "God bless my soul!" said I, "will
wonders never cease?—are there to be no limits to man's
spirit of invention?—is he to invade the very realms of the
immortal, and presume to guide and control the great pas-
sions, the impalpable essences, that have hitherto dwelt in the
secret chambers of the soul, sacred from all save divine in-
trusion?"

I read and re-read that remarkable sign with constantly-
increasing wonder and interest. There was nothing extraordinary in the appearance of the establishment, and even if it
had possessed anything of a supernatural air, it must necessarily have been neutralized by the worldly and substantial
look of a pyramid of excellent bread that stood in the window
—a sign very inconsistent, it seemed to me, with the character of a place devoted to the high and holy employment of
instilling the passion of love into the human heart, although
it was certainly in keeping with the atrocious taste which was
capable of conferring upon a vice-royalty of itself such an

This is the first printing of this story with this title and introduction.—EDITOR.

execrable name as "Love's Bakery." Why not Love's Bower, or the Temple of Love, or the Palace of Cupid?—anything—anything in the world would have been less repulsive than such hideous vulgarity of nomenclature as "Love's *Bakery*."

The place seemed very complete, and well supplied with every facility for carrying on the business of creating love successfully. In a window of the second story was a large tin cage with a parrot in it, and near it was a sign bearing the inscription, "Preparatory School for Young Ladies"—that is, of course, a school where they are taught certain things necessary to prepare them for the bakery down below. Not far off is also a "Preparatory School for Young Gentlemen," which is doubtless connected with Love's Bakery too. I saw none of the pupils of either of the schools, but my imagination dwelt upon them with a deep and friendly interest. How irksome, I thought, must this course of instruction be to these tender hearts, so impatient to be baked into a state of perfect love!

Greatly moved by the singular circumstances which surrounded me, I fell into a profound and pleasing reverie. Here, I thought, they take a couple of hopeful hearts in the rough, and work them up, with spices and shortening and sweetening enough to last for a lifetime, and turn them out well kneaded together, baked to a turn, and ready for matrimony, and without having been obliged to undergo a long and harrowing courtship, with the desperate chances attendant thereon, of persevering rivals, unwilling parents, inevitable love-quarrels and all that sort of thing.

Here, I thought, they will bake you up a couple in moderate circumstances, at short notice and at a cheap rate, and turn them out in good enough shape for the money, perhaps, but nevertheless burnt with the fire of jealousy on one side, and flabby and "duffy" with lukewarmness and indifference on the other, and spotted all over with the saleratus stains of a predisposition to make the conjugal cake bitter and unpalatable for all time to come.

Or they will take an excessively patrician pair, charge them a dozen prices, and deliver them to order in a week, all plastered over with the ghostly vines and flowers of blighted fancies, hopes and yearnings, wrought in chilly ice-work.

Or, perhaps, they will take a brace of youthful, tender hearts, and dish them up in no time, into crisp, delicate "lady-fingers," tempting to contemplate, and suggestive of that serene after-dinner happiness and sociability that come when the gross substantials have been swept from the board and are forgotten in soft dalliance with pastry and ices and sparkling Moselle.

Or maybe they will take two flinty old hearts that have harbored selfishness, envy and all uncharitableness in solitude for half a century, and after a fortnight's roasting, turn them out the hardest kind of hard-tack, invulnerable to all softening influences for evermore.

Here was a revolution far more extended, and destined to be attended by more momentous consequences to the nations of the earth, than any ever projected or accomplished by the greatest of the world's military heroes! Love, the master passion of the human heart, which, since the morning of the creation had shaped the destinies of emperors and beggars alike, and had ruled all men as with a rod of iron, was to be hurled from the seat of power in a single instant, as it were, and brought into subjection to the will of an inspired, a sublimely-gifted baker! By some mysterious magic, by some strange and awful invention, the divine emotion was to be confined within set bounds and limits, controlled, weighed, measured, and doled out to God's creatures in quantities and qualities to suit the purchaser, like vulgar beer and candles!

And in times to come, I thought, the afflicted lover, instead of reading Heuston & Hastings' omnipresent sign and gathering no comfort from it, will read "Go to Love's Bakery!" on the dead-walls and telegraph poles, and be saved.

Now I might never have published to the world my discovery of this manufactory of the human affections in a populous thoroughfare of San Francisco, if it had not occurred to me that some account of it would serve as a peculiarly fitting introductory to a story of love and misfortune, which it falls to my lot to relate. And yet even Love's Bakery could afford no help to the sufferers of whom I shall speak, for they do not lack affection for each other, but are the victims of an accumulation of distressing circumstances against which the efforts of that august agent would be powerless.

The facts in the case come to me by letter from a young lady who lives in the beautiful city of San Jose; she is personally unknown to me, and simply signs herself "Aurelia Maria," which may possibly be a fictitious name. But no matter, the poor girl is almost heart-broken by the misfortunes she has undergone, and so confused by the conflicting counsels of misguided friends and insidious enemies, that she does not know what course to pursue in order to extricate herself from the web of difficulties in which she seems almost hopelessly involved. In this dilemma she turns to me for help, and supplicates for my guidance and instruction with a moving eloquence that would touch the heart of a statue. Hear her sad story:

She says that when she was sixteen years old she met and loved with all the devotion of a passionate nature a young man from New Jersey, named Williamson Breckinridge Caruthers, who was some six years her senior. They were engaged, with the free consent of their friends and relatives, and for a time it seemed as if their career was destined to be characterized by an immunity from sorrow beyond the usual lot of humanity. But at last the tide of fortune turned; young Caruthers became infected with small-pox of the most virulent type, and when he recovered from his illness, his face was pitted like a waffle-mould and his comeliness gone forever. Aurelia thought to break off the engagement at first, but pity for her unfortunate lover caused her to postpone the marriage day for a season, and give him another trial. The very day before the wedding was to have taken place, Breckinridge, while absorbed in watching the flight of a balloon, walked into a well and fractured one of his legs, and it had to be taken off above the knee. Again Aurelia was moved to break the engagement, but again love triumphed, and she set the day forward and gave him another chance to reform. And again misfortune overtook the unhappy youth. He lost one arm by the premature discharge of a Fourth-of-July cannon, and within three months he got the other pulled out by a carding-machine. Aurelia's heart was almost crushed by these latter calamities. She could not but be deeply grieved to see her lover passing from her by piecemeal, feeling, as she did, that he could not last forever under this disastrous process of reduction, yet knowing of no way to stop its dreadful career, and in her tearful despair she almost regretted, like brokers who hold on and lose, that she had not taken him at first, before he had suffered such an alarming depreciation. Still, her brave soul bore her up, and she resolved to bear with her friend's unnatural disposition yet a little longer. Again the wedding-day approached, and again disappointment overshadowed it. Caruthers fell ill with the erysipelas, and lost the use of one of his eyes entirely. The friends and relatives of the bride, considering that she had already put up with more than could reasonably be expected of her, now came forward and insisted that the match should be broken off; but after wavering awhile, Aurelia, with a generous spirit which did her credit, said she had reflected calmly upon the matter and could not discover that Breckinridge was to blame. So she extended the time once more, and he broke his other leg. It was a sad day for the poor girl when she saw the surgeons reverently bearing away the sack whose uses she had learned by previous experience, and her heart told her the bitter truth that some more of her lover was gone. She felt that the field of her affections was growing more and more circumscribed every day, but once more she frowned down her relatives and renewed her betrothal. Shortly before the time set for the nuptials another disaster occurred. There was but one man scalped by the Owens River Indians last year. That man was Williamson Breckinridge Caruthers, of New Jersey. He was hurrying home with happiness in his heart, when he lost his hair forever, and in that hour of bitterness he almost cursed the mistaken mercy that had spared his head.

At last Aurelia is in serious perplexity as to what she ought to do. She still loves her Breckinridge, she writes, with true womanly feeling—she still loves what is left of him—but her parents are bitterly opposed to the match, because he has no property and is disabled from working, and she has not sufficient means to support both comfortably. "Now, what should she do?" she asks with painful and anxious solicitude.

It is a delicate question; it is one which involves the life-long happiness of a woman, and that of nearly two-thirds of a man, and I feel that it would be assuming too great a responsibility to do more than make a mere suggestion in the case. How would it do to build to him? If Aurelia can afford the expense, let her furnish her mutilated lover with wooden arms and wooden legs, and a glass eye and a wig, and give him another show; give him ninety days, without grace, and if he does not break his neck in the meantime, marry him and take the chances. It does not seem to me that there is much risk, any way, because if he sticks to his infernal propensity for damaging himself every time he sees a good opportunity, his next experiment is bound to finish him, and then you are all right, you know, married or single. If married, the wooden legs and such other valuables as he may possess, revert to the widow, and you see you sustain no actual loss save the cherished fragment of a noble but most unfortunate husband, who honestly strove to do right, but whose extraordinary instincts were against him. Try it, Maria! I have thought the matter over carefully and well, and it is the only chance I see for you. It would have been a happy conceit on the part of Caruthers if he had started with his neck and broken that first, but since he has seen fit to choose a different policy and string

himself out as long as possible, I do not think we ought to up-
braid him for it if he has enjoyed it. We must do the best we
can under the circumstances, and try not to feel exasperated
at him.   MARK TWAIN.

CALIFORNIAN, *October* 22, 1864.

CHAPTER V

Daniel in the Lion's Den—and Out Again All Right

SOME PEOPLE are not particular about what sort of company they keep. I am one of that kind. Now for several days I have been visiting the Board of Brokers, and associating with brokers, and drinking with them, and swapping lies with them, and being as familiar and sociable with them as I would with the most respectable people in the world. I do this because I consider that a broker goes according to the instincts that are in him, and means no harm, and fulfils his mission according to his lights, and has a right to live, and be happy in a general way, and be protected by the law to some extent, just the same as a better man. I consider that brokers come into the world with souls—I am satisfied they do; and if they wear them out in the course of a long career of stock-jobbing, have they not a right to come in at the eleventh hour and get themselves half-soled, like old boots, and be saved at last? Certainly—the father of the tribe did that, and do we say anything against Barabbas for it to-day? No! we concede his right to do it; we admire his mature judgment in selling out of a worked-out mine of iniquity and investing in righteousness, and no man denies, or even doubts, the validity of the transaction. Other people may think as they please, and I suppose I am entitled to the same privilege; therefore, notwithstanding what others may believe, I am of the opinion that a broker can be saved. Mind, I do not say that a broker *will* be saved, or even that is uncommon likely that such a thing will happen—I only say that Lazarus was raised from the dead, the five thousand were fed with twelve loaves of bread, the water was turned into wine, the Israelites crossed the Red Sea dry-shod, and a broker *can* be saved. True, the angel that accomplishes the task may require all eternity to rest himself in, but has that got anything to do with the establishment of the proposition? Does it invalidate it? does it detract from it? I think not. I am aware that this enthusiastic and may-be highly-colored vindication of the brokers may lay me open to suspicion of bribery, but I care not; I am a native of Washoe, and I will stand by anybody that stands by Washoe.

The place where stocks are daily bought and sold is called by interested parties the Hall of the San Francisco Board of Brokers, but by the impartial and disinterested the Den of the Forty Thieves; the latter name is regarded as the most poetic, but the former is considered the most polite. The large room is well stocked with small desks, arranged in semi-circular ranks like the seats of an amphitheatre, and behind these sit the th—the brokers. The portly President, with his gavel of office in his hand, an abundance of whiskers and moustaches on his face, spectacles on nose, an expression of energy and decision on his countenance and an open plaza on his head, sits, with his three clerks, in a pulpit at the head of the hall, flanked on either hand by two large cases, with glass doors, containing mineralogical specimens from Washoe and California mines—the emblems of the traffic. Facing the President, at the opposite end of the hall, is a blackboard, whereon is written in accusing capitals, "John Smith delinquent to John Jones, $1,550; William Brown delinquent to Jonas White, $475!' You might think brokers wouldn't mind that, maybe, but they do; a delinquent loses caste, and that touches his fine moral sensibilities—and he is suspended from active membership for the time being, and even expelled if his delinquency savors of blundering and ungraceful rascality—a thing which the Board cannot abide—and this inflicts exquisite pain upon the delicate nerves and tissues of his pocket, now when a seat in the Den is worth twelve or fifteen hundred dollars, and in brisker times even three thousand.

The session of the Board being duly opened, the roll is rapidly called, the members present responding, and the absentees being noted by the clerks for fines:

"Ackerman, (Here!) Adams, Atchison, (Here!) Babcock, Bocock, (Here!) Badger, Blitzen, Bulger, Buncombe, (Here!) Caxton, (Here!) Cobbler, Crowder, Clutterback, (Here!) Dashaway, Dilson, Dodson, Dummy (Here!)"—and so on, the place becoming lively and animated, and the members sharpening their pencils, disposing their printed stock-lists before them, and getting ready for a sowing of unrighteousness and a harvest of sin.

In a few moments the roll-call was finished, the pencils all sharpened, and the brokers prepared for business—some with a leg thrown negligently over the arms of their chairs, some tilted back comfortably with their knees against their desks, some sitting half upright and glaring at the President, hungry for the contention to begin—but not a rascal of them tapping his teeth with his pencil—only dreamy, absent-minded people do that.

Then the President called "Ophir!" and after some bidding and counter-bidding, "Gould and Curry!" and a Babel arose —an infernal din and clatter of all kinds and tones of voices, inextricably jumbled together like original chaos, and above it all the following observation by the President pealed out clearly and distinctly, and with a rapidity of enunciation that was amazing:

"Fift'naitassfrwahn fift'nseftfive bifferwahn fift'naitfive botherty!"

I said I believed I would go home. My broker friend who had procured my admission to the Board asked why I wanted to go so soon, and I was obliged to acknowledge to him that I was very unfamiliar with the Kanaka language, and could not understand it at all unless a man spoke it exceedingly slow and deliberately.

"Oh," said he, "sit still; that isn't Kanaka; it's English, but he talks so fast and runs one word into another; it is easy SOLD! to understand when you GIVE FIFTEEN-NINETY BUYER TEN NO DEPOSIT! come to get used to it. He always talks so, and sometimes he says THAT'S MINE! JIGGERS SOLD ON SLAD-DERY'S BID! his words so fast that even some of the members cannot comprehend them readily. Now what he said then was NO SIR! I DIDN'T SAY BUYER THIRTY, I SAID REGULAR WAY! 'Fifteen-eighty, (meaning fifteen hundred and eighty dollars,) asked for one, (one foot,) fifteen-seventy-five bid for one, fifteen-eighty-five buyer thirty,' (thirty days' time on the payment,) 'TWASN'T MY BID, IT WAS SWIGGINS TO BAB-COCK! and he was repeating the bids and offers of the members after them as fast as they were made. I'LL TAKE IT, CASH!"

I felt relieved, but not enlightened. My broker's explana-tion had got so many strange and incomprehensible interpola-tions sandwiched into it that I began to look around for a suitable person to translate that for me also, when it occurred to me that those interpolations were bids, offers, etc., which he had been throwing out to the assembled brokers while he was talking to me. It was all clear, then, so I have put his side-remarks in small capitals so that they may be clear to the reader likewise, and show that they have no connection with the subject matter of my friend's discourse.

And all this time, the clatter of voices had been going on. And while the storm of ejaculations hurtled about their heads, these brokers sat calmly in their several easy attitudes, but when a sale was made—when, in answer to some particularly liberal bid, somebody sung out "SOLD!" down came legs from the arms of chairs, down came knees propped against desks, forward shot the heads of the whole tribe with one ac-cord, and away went the long ranks of pencils dancing over the paper! the sale duly recorded by all, the heads, the legs and the knees came up again, and the negligent attitudes were resumes once more.

The din moderated now, somewhat, and for awhile only a random and desultory fire was kept up as the President drifted down the stock-list, calling at intervals, "Savage!" "Uncle Sam!" "Chollar!" "Potosi!" "Hale and Norcross!" "Imperial!" "Sierra Nevada!" "Daney!" the monotony being broken and the uncomfortable attitudes demolished, now and then, by a lucky chance-shot that went to the mark and made a sale. But when the old gentleman called "Burning Moscow!" you should have seen the fiends wake up! you should have heard the racket! you should have been there to behold the metaphorical bull in the China shop! The President's voice and his mallet went into active service, then, and mingled their noise with the clamors of the mob. The members thus:

"Sell ten forty-five cash!" "Give forty-three for ten, regular way!" "Give forty-one cash for any part fifty!" "Twenty thirty-eight seller sixty!" "Give forty-four for ten buyer thirty!" "SOLD!" (Down with your legs again, forward with your heads, and out with your pencils!) "Sell ten forty-three cash!" "Sold!" Then from every part of the house a din like this: "Ten more!" "Sold!" "Ten more!" "Sold!" "Ten more!" "Sold!" "Ten more!" "Sold!" "Ten—"

President (rap with his gavel)—Silence! Orfuplease, (order if you please,) gentlemen! Higgins ten to Smithers—Dodson ten to Snodgrass—"

Billson—"No, sir! Billson ten to Snodgrass! It was me that sold 'em, sir!"

Dodson—"I didn't sell, sir, I bought—Jiggers ten to Dodson!"

President—"Billson ten to Snodgrass—Jiggers ten to Dodson—Slushbuster ten to Bladders—Simpson ten to Blivens—Guttersnipe ten to Hogwash—aw-right! go on!"

And they did go on, hotter and heavier than ever. And as they yelled their terms, the President repeated after them—

the words flowing in a continuous stream from his mouth with inconceivable rapidity, and melting and mingling together like bottle-glass and cinders after a conflagration:

"Fortwahnasscash fortray bidbortenn fortsix botherty fortsevnoffsetherty fortfourbiffertenn—(smash! with the gavel) whasthat?—aw right! fortfive offranparfortbotherty nodeposit fortfivenaf botherty bid fortsix biglerway!"

Which, translated, means: "Forty-one asked, cash; forty-three bid, buyer ten; forty-six, buyer thirty; forty-seven offered, seller thirty; forty-four bid for ten—(pause)—What's that? All right—forty-five offered for any part of forty, buyer thirty, no deposit; forty-five and a half, buyer thirty, bid; forty-six bid, regular way!"

And I found out that a "Bull" is a broker who raises the market-price of a stock by every means in his power, and a "Bear" is one who depresses it; that "cash" means that the stock must be delivered and paid for immediately—that is, before the banks close; that "regular way" means that delivery of the stock and payment must be made within two days; that it is the seller who "offers" stock, and the buyer who "bids" for it; that "buyer ten, thirty," or whatever the specified number may be, signifies the number of days the purchaser is allowed in which to call for the stock, receive it and pay for it, and it implies also that he must deposit in somebody's hands a fifth part of the price of the stock purchased, to be forfeited to the seller in case the full payment is not made within the time set—full payment must be made, though, notwithstanding the forfeit, or the broker loses his seat if the seller makes complaint to the Board within forty-eight hours after the occurrence of the delinquency; that when the words "no deposit" are added to "buyer thirty," they imply that the twenty per cent. deposit is not to be made, of course; that "seller thirty" means that any time the seller chooses, during the thirty days, he can present the stock to the buyer and demand payment—the seller generally selling at a figure below the market rate, in the hope that before his time is up a depression may occur that will enable him to pick up the stock at half price and deliver it—and the buyer taking chances on a great advance, within the month, that will accrue to his profit. Think of one of these adventurous "seller thirty's" "selling short," at thirty dollars a foot, several feet of a stock that was all corralled and withdrawn from the market within a fortnight and went to about fifteen hundred! It is not worth while to mention names—I suppose you remember the circumstance.

But I digress. Sometimes on the "second call" of stocks—that is, after the list has been gone through with in regular order, and the members are privileged to call up any stock they please—strategy is driven to the utmost limit by the friends of some pet wildcat or other, to effect sales of it to disinterested parties. The seller "offers" at a high figure, and the "bidder" responds with a low one; then the former comes warily down a dollar at a time, and the latter approaches him from below at about the same rate; they come nearer and nearer, skirmish a little in close proximity, get to a point where another bid or another offer would commit the parties to a sale, and then in the imminence of the impending event the seller hesitates a second and is silent. But behold! as has been said of Woman, "The Broker that hesitates is lost!" The nervous and impatient President can brook no silence, no delay, and calls out: "Awstock?" (Any other stock?) Somebody yells "Burning Moscow!" and the tender wildcat, almost born, miscarries. Or perhaps the skirmishers fight shyly up to each other, counter and cross-counter, feint and parry, back and fill, and finally clinch a sale in the center—the bidder is bitten, a smile flits from face to face, down come the legs, forward the ranks of heads, the pencils charge on the stock-lists, and the neat transaction is recorded with a rare gusto.

But twelve pages of foolscap are warning me to cut this thrilling sketch short, notwithstanding it is only half finished. However, I cannot leave the subject without saying I was agreeably disappointed in those brokers; I expected to see a set of villains with the signs of total depravity hung out all over them, but now I am satisfied there is some good in them; that they are not entirely and irredeemably bad; and I have been told by a friend, whose judgment I respect, that they are not any more unprincipled than they look. This was said by a man who would scorn to stoop to flattery. At the same time, though, as I scanned the faces assembled in that hall, I could not help imagining I could see old St. Peter admitting that band of Bulls and Bears into Paradise—see him standing by the half-open gate with his ponderous key pressed thoughtfully against his nose, and his head canted critically to one side, as he looks after them tramping down the gold-paved avenue, and mutters to himself: "Well, *you're* a nice lot, any way! Humph! I think you'll find it sort of lonesome in heaven, for if my judgment is sound, you'll not find a good many of *your* stripe in there!"   MARK TWAIN.

CALIFORNIAN, *November* 5, 1864.

CHAPTER VI

A Full and Reliable Account of the Extraordinary Meteoric Shower of Last Saturday Night

I FOUND the following paragraph in the morning papers of the 11th inst.:

VIRGINIA, November 10.—Astronomers anticipate a recurrence this year of the November meteoric shower of 1833. The mornings from the 11th to the 15th are all likely to show an unusual number of meteors, especially from the 12th to the 14th. The best time of observation is from half-past one o'clock, A. M., onward. The radiant point is the constellation Leo. Observers in California, Nevada and the Pacific Coast generally, are requested to report their observations to Professor Silliman, Jr., San Francisco, for the *American Journal of Science*, where they will be published for the good of science. B. SILLIMAN, JR.

PROF. B. SILLIMAN, JR.—*Dear Sir:* In accordance with the above request, which you so politely extended to all "observers," I took copious notes of the amazing meteoric phenomena of last Saturday night, and I now hasten to make my report to you for publication in the *American Journal of Science* "for the good of science."

I began my observations early in the evening, previously providing myself with the very best apparatus I could find wherewith to facilitate my labors. I got a telescopic glass tumbler, and two costly decanters, (containing *eau de vie* and Veuve Cliquot to wash out the instrument with whenever it should become clouded), and seated myself in my window, very nearly under the constellation Leo. I then poured about a gill of liquid from each decanter into the telescopic tumbler and slowly elevated it to an angle of about ninety degrees. I did not see anything. The second trial was also a failure, but I had faith in that wash, and I washed out the instrument again. And just here let me suggest to you, Professor, that you can always depend on that mixture; rightly compounded, I expect it is the most powerful aid to human eyesight ever invented; assisted by it I have known a man to see two drinks on the counter before him when in reality there was but one—and so strong was the deception that I have known that man to get drunk on thirteen of these duplicate drinks when he was naturally gauged for twenty-six.

Very well; after I had washed out my glass the third time, three or four stars, of about the nineteenth magnitude, I should judge, shot from the zenith and fell in the general direction of Oakland. During the fourth wash, and while I had one eye sighted on Venus and the other one closed in blissful repose, that planet fell upon the roof of the Russ House and bounced off into Bush street; immediately afterward, Jupiter fell and knocked a watchman's eye out—at least I think it was that star, because I saw the watchman clap his hand to his eye and say "By Jupiter!" The assertion was positive, and made without hesitation, as if he had the most perfect confidence in the accuracy of his judgment; but at the same time it is possible that he might have been mistaken, and that the damage was not done by Jupiter after all. I maintain, though, that the chances are all in favor of his being correct, because I have noticed that policemen usually know as much about stars as anybody, and take more interest in them than most people.

Up to this time the wind had been north by northeast half west, and I noticed an uncommon dryness in the atmosphere, but it was less marked after I applied the fifth wash. My barometer never having had any experience in falling stars, got hopelessly tangled in trying to get the run of things, and after waltzing frantically between "stormy" and "falling weather" for awhile without being able to make up its mind, it finally became thoroughly demoralized and threw up its commission. My thermometer did not indicate anything; I noted this extraordinary phenomenon, of course, but at the same time I reasoned—and, I think, with considerable sagacity—that it was less owing to the singular condition of the atmosphere than to the fact that there was no quicksilver in the instrument. About this time a magnificent spectacle dazzled my vision—the whole constellation of the Great Menken came flaming out of the heavens like a vast spray of gas-jets, and shed a glory abroad over the universe as it fell! [N. B. I have used the term "Great Menken" because I regard it as a more modest expression than the Great Bear, and consequently better suited to the columns of THE CALIFORNIAN, which goes among families, you understand—but when you come to transfer my report to the *Journal of Science*, Professor, you are at liberty to change it if you like.]

I applied the sixth wash. A sprinkle of sparkling fragments ensued—fragments of some beautiful world that had been broken up and cast out of the blue firmament—and then a radiance of noonday flared out of the zenith, and Mercury, the winged symbol of Progress, came sweeping down like a banished sun, and catching in the folds of the flag that floats from the tall staff in the Plaza, remained blazing in the centre of its dim constellation of stars! "Lo, a miracle! the thirty-sixth star furnished from the imperial diadem of heaven! while yet no welcome comes from the old home in the Orient, behold the STATE OF NEVADA is recognized by God!" says I, and seized my telescope, filled her to the brim and washed her out again! The divinity student in the next room came in at this juncture and protested against my swearing with so much spirit, and I had some difficulty in making him understand that I had only made use of a gorgeous metaphor, and that there was really no profanity intended in it.

About this time the wind changed and quite a shower of stars fell, lasting about twenty minutes; a lull ensued, and then came several terrific discharges of thunder and lightning, and how it poured! you couldn't see the other side of the street for the hurtling tempest of stars! I got my umbrella—which I had previously provided along with my other apparatus—and started down the street. Of course there was plenty of light, although the street lamps were not lit—(you let that sagacious gas company alone, Professor, to make a good thing out of it when the almanac advertises anything of this kind. I put in these parentheses to signify a complicated wink—you understand?) I met Charles Kean, and I expect he was drunk; I drifted down the pavement, tacking from one side of it to the other, and trying to give him a wide berth, but it was no use; he would run into me, and he did—he brought up square against me and fell. "Down goes another star," I observed and stopped a moment to make a note of it.

The meteoric storm abated gradually, and finally ceased, but by that time the stars had cut my umbrella nearly all to pieces, and there were a dozen or more sticking in it when I lowered it. It was the most furious deluge I ever saw, while it lasted. Pretty soon I heard a great huzzaing in the distance, and immediately afterward I noticed a brilliant meteor streaming athwart the heavens with a train of fire of incredible length appended to it. It swept the sky in a graceful curve, and after I had watched its splendid career a few seconds and was in the act of making the proper entry in my note-book, it descended and struck me such a stunning thump in the pit of the stomach that I was groveling in the dust before I rightly knew what the matter was. When I recovered consciousness, I remarked "Down went a couple of us then," and made a note of it. I saved the remains of this most remarkable meteor, and I transmit them to you with this report, to be preserved in the National Astronomical Museum. They consist of a fragment of a torn and jagged cylinder the size of your wrist, composed of a substance strongly resembling the pasteboard of this world; to this is attached a slender stick some six feet long, which has something of the appearance of the pine wood so well known to the commerce of this earth, but of such a supernatural fineness of texture, of course, as to enable one to detect its celestial origin at once. There is food here for philosophic contemplation, and a series of interesting volumes might be written upon a question which I conceive to be of the utmost importance to Science, viz.: Do they cultivate pines in Paradise? And if it be satisfactorily demonstrated that they *do* cultivate pines in Paradise, may we not reasonably surmise that they cultivate cabbages there also? O, sublime thought! O, beautiful dream! The scientific world may well stand speechless and awe-stricken in the presence of these tremendous questions! But may we not hope that the learned German who has devoted half his valuable life to determining what materials a butterfly's wing is made of, and to writing unstinted books upon the subject, will devote the balance of it to profound investigation of the celestial cabbage question? And is it too much to hope that that other benefactor of our race who has proven in his thirteen inspired volumes that it is exceedingly mixed as to whether the extraordinary bird called the Phœnix ever really existed or not, will lend his assistance to the important work and turn out a few tomes upon the subject, wherewith to enrich our scientific literature? My dear sir, this matter is worthy of the noblest effort; for we know by the past experience of learned men, that whosoever shall either definitely settle this cabbage question, or indefinitely unsettle it with arguments and reasonings and deductions freighted with that odor of stately and incomprehensible wisdom which is so overpowering to the aspiring student and so dazzling and bewildering to the world at large, will be clothed with titles of dignity by our colleges, and receive medals of gold from the Kings and Presidents of the earth.

As I was meandering down the street, pondering over the matters treated of in the preceding paragraph, I ran against another man, and he squared off for a fight. I squared off, also, and dashed out with my left, but he dodged and "cross-countered." [I have since learned that he was educated at the

Olympic Club.] That is to say, he ducked his head to one side and avoided my blow, and at the same time he let go with his right and caved the side of my head in. At this moment I beheld the most magnificent discharge of stars that had occurred during the whole evening. I estimated the number to be in the neighborhood of fifteen hundred thousand. I beg that you will state it at that figure in the *Journal of Science*, Professor, and throw in a compliment about my wasting no opportunity that seemed to promise anything for the good of the cause. It might help me along with your kind of men if I should conclude to tackle science for a regular business, you know. You see they have elected a new Governor over there in Nevada, and consequently I am not as much Governor of the Third House there as I was. It was a very comfortable berth; I had a salary of $60,000 a year when I could collect it.

While my stranger and myself were staggering under the two terrific blows which we had exchanged—and especially myself, on account of the peculiar nature of the "cross-counter" as above described—a singular star dropped in our midst which I would have liked well to possess, because of its quaint appearance, and because I had never seen anything like it mentioned in Mr. Dick's astronomy. It emitted a mild silvery lustre, and bore upon its face some characters which, in the fervor of my astronomical enthusiasm, I imagined spelt "Police—18," but of course this was an absurd delusion. I only mention it to show to what lengths scientific zeal will sometimes carry a novice. This marvellous meteor was already in the possession of another enthusiast, and he would not part with it.

On my way home, I met young John William Skae—the inimitable punster of Virginia City, and formerly of Pennsylvania, perhaps you know him?—and I knew from his distraught and pensive air that he was building a joke. I was anxious not to intrude any excitement upon him, which might have the effect of bringing the half-finished edifice down about my ears, but my very caution precipitated the catastrophe I was trying to avert. Said I, "Are you out looking for meteors, too?" His eye instantly lighted with a devilish satisfaction, and says he: "Well, sorter; I'm looking for my Susan —going to meteor by moonlight alone; O Heavens! why this sudden pang, this bursting brain! save me, save me or I perish!"

But I didn't save him—I let him drop; and I deserted him and left him moaning there in the gutter. A man cannot serve me that way twice and expect me to stand by him and chafe his temples and blow his nose and sand-paper his legs and fetch him round again. I would let him perish like an outcast first, and deny him Christian burial afterwards. That Skae has always been following me around trying to make me low-spirited with his dismal jokes, but since that time he caught me out in the lonely moor on the Cliff House road, and intimidated me into listening to that execrable pun on the King-fisher, I have avoided him as I would a pestilence.

I will now close my report, Professor. If you had not just happened to print that assurance in your little notice that these things should be published in the *American Journal of Science*, "for the good of Science," I expect it never would have occurred to me to make any meteorological observations at all; but you see that remark corralled me. It has been the dearest wish of my life to do something for the good of Science and see it in print in such a paper as the one you mention, and when I saw this excellent opportunity presented, I thought it was now or never with me. It is a pity that the astonishing drawings which accompany this report cannot be published in The Californian; it could not be helped, though: the artist who was to have engraved them was not healthy, and he only took one look at them and then went out in the back yard and destroyed himself. But you can print them in the *Journal of Science*, anyhow, just the same; get an artist whose sensibilities have been toned down by chiseling melancholy devices on tombstones all his life, and let him do them up for you. He would probably survive the job.　Mark Twain.

Californian, *November* 19, 1864.

CHAPTER VII

An Unbiased Criticism

THE CALIFORNIA ART UNION—ITS MORAL EFFECTS UPON THE YOUTH OF
BOTH SEXES CAREFULLY CONSIDERED AND CANDIDLY COMMENTED UPON.

THE Editor of THE CALIFORNIAN ordered me to go to the rooms of the California Art Union and write an elaborate criticism upon the pictures upon exhibition there, and I beg leave to report that the result is hereunto appended together with bill for same.

I do not know anything about Art and very little about music or anatomy, but nevertheless I enjoy looking at pictures and listening to operas, and gazing at handsome young girls, about the same as people do who are better qualified by education to judge of merit in these matters.

After writing the above rather neat heading and preamble on my foolscap, I proceeded to the new Art Union rooms last week, to see the paintings, about which I had read so much in the papers during my recent three months' stay in the Big Tree region of Calaveras county; [up there, you know, they read *everything*, because in most of those little camps they have no libraries, and no books to speak of, except now and then a patent-office report, or a prayer-book, or literature of that kind, in a general way, that will hang on and last a good while when people are careful with it, like miners; but as for novels, they pass them around and wear them out in a week or two. Now there was Coon, a nice bald-headed man at the hotel in Angels' Camp, I asked him to lend me a book, one rainy day: he was silent a moment, and a shade of melancholy flitted across his fine face, and then he said: "Well, I've got a mighty responsible old Webster-Unabridged, what there is left of it, but they started her sloshing around, and sloshing around, and sloshing around the camp before I ever got a chance to read her myself, and next she went to Murphy's, and from there she went to Jackass, and now, by G—d, she's gone to San Andreas, and I don't expect I'll ever see that book again; but what makes me mad, is that for all they're so handy about keeping her sashshaying around from shanty to shanty and from camp to camp, none of 'em's ever got a good word for her. Now Coddington had her a week, and she was too much for *him*—he couldn't spell the words; he tackled some of them regular busters, tow'rd the middle, you know, and they throwed him; next, Dyer, *he* tried her a jolt, but he couldn't *pronounce* 'em—Dyer can hunt quail or play seven-up as well as any man, understand me, but he can't *pronounce* worth a d—n; he used to worry along well enough, though, till he'd flush one of them rattlers with a clatter of syllables as long as a string of sluice-boxes, and then he'd lose his grip and throw up his hand; and so, finally, Dick Stoker harnessed her, up there at his cabin, and sweated over her, and cussed over her, and rastled with her for as much as three weeks, night and day, till he got as far as R, and then passed her over to 'Lige Pickerell, and said she was the all-firedest dryest reading that ever *he* struck; well, well, if she's come back from San Andreas, you can get her and prospect her, but I don't reckon there's a good deal left of her by this time; though time was when she was as likely a book as any in the State, and as hefty, and had an amount of general information in her that was astonishing, if any of these cattle had known enough to get it out of her;" and ex-corporal Coon proceeded cheerlessly to scout with his brush after the straggling hairs on the rear of his head and drum them to the front for inspection and roll-call, as was his usual custom before turning in for his regular afternoon nap]: but as I was saying, they read everything, up there, and consequently all the Art criticisms, and the "Parlor Theatricals *vs.* Christian Commission" controversy, and even the quarrels in the advertising columns between rival fire-proof safe and sewing machine companies were devoured with avidity. Why, they eventually became divided on these questions, and discussed them with a spirit of obstinacy and acrimony that I have seldom seen equalled in the most important religious and political controversies. I have known a Grover & Baker fanatic to cut his own brother dead because he went for the Florence. As you have already guessed, perhaps, the county and township elections were carried on these issues alone, almost. I took sides, of course—every man had to—there was no shirking the responsibility; a man must be one thing or the other, either Florence or Grover & Baker, unless, of course, he chose to side with some outside machine faction, strong enough to be somewhat formidable. I was a bitter Florence man, and I think my great speech in the bar-room of the Union Hotel, at Angels', on the night of the 13th of February, will long be remembered as the deadliest blow the unprincipled Grover & Baker cabal ever got in that camp, and as having done more to thwart their hellish designs upon the liberties of our beloved country than any single effort of any one man that was ever made in that county. And in that same speech I administered a scathing rebuke to the "*Lillie Union and Constitution Fire and Burglar Proof Safe Party,*" (for I was a malignant Tilton & McFarland man and would break bread and eat salt with none other), that made even the most brazen among them blush for the infamous and damnable designs they had hatched and were still hatching against the Palladium of Freedom in Calaveras county. The concluding passage of my speech was considered to have been the finest display of eloquence and power ever heard in that part of the country, from Rawhide Ranch to Deadhorse Flat. I said:

"FELLOW-CITIZENS: A word more, and I am done. Men of Calaveras—men of Cuyote Flat—men of Jackass—BEWARE

OF CODDINGTON! [Cheers.] Beware of this atrocious ditch-owner—this vile water-rat—this execrable dry-land shrimp—this bold and unprincipled mud-turtle, who sells water to Digger, Chinaman, Greaser and American alike, and at the self-same prices—who would sell you, who would sell me, who would sell us ALL, to carry out the destructive schemes of the *'Enlightened* [Bah!] *Freedom & Union Grover & Baker Loop-Stitch Sewing Machine Party* [groans] of which wretched conglomeration of the ruff-scruff and rag-tag-and-bob-tail of noble old Calaveras he is the appropriate leader—BEWAR-R-E of him! [Tremendous applause.] Again I charge you as men whom future generations will hold to a fearful responsibility, to BEWARE OF CODDINGTON! [Tempests of applause.] Beware of this unsavory remnant of a once pure and high-minded man!* [Renewed applause.] Beware of this faithless modern Esau, who would sell his birthright of freedom and ours, for a mess of pottage!—for a mess of tripe!—for a mess of sauer-kraut and garlic!—for a mess of anything under the sun that a Christian Florence Patriot would scorn and a Digger Indian turn from with loathing and disgust!† [Thunders of applause.] Remember Coddington on election day! and remember him but to damn him! I appeal to you, sovereign and enlightened Calaverasses, and my heart tells me that I do not appeal in vain! I have done. [Earthquakes of applause that made the welkin tremble for many minutes, and finally died away in hoarse demands for the villain Coddington, and threats to lynch him.]

I felt exhausted, and in need of rest after my great effort, and so I tore myself from my enthusiastic friends and went home with Coddington to his hospitable mansion, where we partook of an excellent supper and then retired to bed, after

---

* He used to belong to the Florence at first.   M. T.

† I grant you that that last part was a sort of a strong figure, seeing that that tribe are not over-particular in the matter of diet, and don't usually go back on anything that they can chaw.   M. T.

playing several games of seven-up for beer and booking some
heavy election bets.

The contest on election day was bitter, and to the last degree exciting, but principles triumphed over party jugglery
and chicanery, and we carried everything but the Constable
(Unconditional Button-Hole Stitch and Anti-Parlor Theatrical candidate), and Tax Collector (Moderate Lillie Fire-
Proof and Fusion Grover & Button-Hole Stitch Machines),
and County Assessor (Radical Christian Commission and
Independent Sewing Machine candidate), and we could have
carried these, also, but at the last moment fraudulent hand-
bills were suddenly scattered abroad containing sworn affidavits that a Tilton & McFarland safe, on its way from New
York, had melted in the tropical sunshine after fifteen minutes' exposure on the Isthmus; also, that the lock stitch, back
stitch, fore-and-aft, forward-and-back, down-the-middle,
double-and-twist, and the other admirable stitches and
things upon which the splendid reputation of the Florence
rests, had all been cabbaged from the traduced and reviled
Button-Hole Stitch and Grover & Baker machines; also, that
so far from the Parlor-Theatrical-Christian-Commission controversy being finished, it had sprung up again in San Francisco, and by latest advices the Opposition was ahead. What
men could do, we did, but although we checked the demorali-
zation that had broken out in our ranks, we failed to carry all
our candidates. We sent express to San Andreas and Colum-
bia, and had strong affidavits—sworn to by myself and our
candidates—printed, denouncing the other publications as
low and disreputable falsehoods and calumnies, whose shameless authors ought to be driven beyond the pale of civilized
society, and winding up with the withering revelation that
the rain had recently soaked through one of Lillie's Fire and
Burglar-Proof safes in San Francisco, and badly damaged the
books and papers in it; and that, in the process of drying, the
safe warped so that the door would not swing on its hinges,
and had to be "prized" open with a butter-knife. O, but that

was a rough shot! It blocked the game and saved the day for
us—and just at the critical moment our reserve (whom we
had sent for and drummed up in Tuolumne and the adjoin-
ing counties, and had kept out of sight and full of chain-
lightning, sudden death and scorpion-bile all day in Tom
Deer's back-yard,) came filing down the street as drunk as
loons, with a drum and fife and lighted transparencies, (day-
light and dark were all the same to *them* in *their* condition),
bearing such stirring devices as:

> "*The Florence is bound to rip, therefore,* LET HER RIP!"
> "*Grover & Baker, how are you* NOW?"
> "*Nothing can keep the Opposition cool in the other world but*
> *Tilton & McFarland's Chilled Iron Safes!*" etc., etc.

A vast Florence machine on wheels led the van, and a sick
Chinaman bearing a crippled Grover & Baker brought up the
rear. The procession reeled up to the polls with deafening
cheers for the Florence and curses for the "loop stitch
scoun'rels," and deposited their votes like men for freedom of
speech, freedom of the press and freedom of conscience in the
matter of sewing machines, provided they are Florences.

I had a very comfortable time in Calaveras county, in spite
of the rain, and if I had my way I would go back there, and
argue the sewing machine question around Coon's bar-room
stove again with the boys on rainy evenings. Calaveras possesses some of the grandest natural features that have ever
fallen under the contemplation of the human mind—such as
the Big Trees, the famous Morgan gold mine which is the
richest in the world at the present time, perhaps, and
"straight" whisky that will throw a man a double somerset
and limber him up like boiled maccaroni before he can set his
glass down. Marvelous and incomprehensible is the straight
whisky of Angels' Camp!

But I digress to some extent, for maybe it was not really
necessary to be quite so elaborate as I have been in order to
enable the reader to understand that we were in the habit of

reading everything thoroughly that fell in our way at Angels, and that consequently we were familiar with all that had appeared in print about the new Art Union rooms. They get all the papers regularly every evening there, 24 hours out from San Francisco.

However, now that I have got my little preliminary point established to my satisfaction, I will proceed with my Art criticism.

The rooms of the California Art Union are pleasantly situated over the picture store in Montgomery street near the Eureka Theatre, and the first thing that attracts your attention when you enter is a beautiful and animated picture representing the Trial Scene in the *Merchant of Venice*. They did not charge me anything for going in there, because the Superintendent was not noticing at the time, but it is likely he would charge you or another man twenty-five cents—I think he would, because when I tried to get a dollar and a half out of a fellow I took for a stranger, the new-comer said the usual price was only two bits, and besides he was a heavy life-member and not obliged to pay anything at all—so I had to let him in for a quarter, but I had the satisfaction of telling him we were not letting life-members in free, now, as much as we *were*. It touched him on the raw. I let another fellow in for nothing, because I had cabined with him a few nights in Esmeralda several years ago, and I thought it only fair to be hospitable with him now that I had a chance. He introduced me to a friend of his named Brown, (I was hospitable to Brown also,) and me and Brown sat down on a bench and had a long talk about Washoe and other things, and I found him very entertaining for a stranger. He said his mother was a hundred and thirteen years old, and he had an aunt who died in her infancy, who, if she had lived, would have been older than his mother, now. He judged so because, originally, his aunt was born before his mother was. That was the first thing he told me, and then we were friends in a moment. It could not but be flattering to me, a stranger to be made the recipient of information of so private and sacred a nature as the age of his mother and the early decease of his aunt, and I naturally felt drawn towards him and bound to him by a stronger and a warmer tie than the cold, formal introduction that had previously passed between us. I shall cherish the memory of the ensuing two hours as being among the purest and happiest of my checkered life. I told him frankly who I was, and where I came from, and where I was going to, and when I calculated to start, and all about my uncle Ambrose, who was an Admiral, and was for a long time in command of a large fleet of canal boats, and about my gifted aunt Martha, who was a powerful poetess, and a dead shot, with a brickbåt at forty yards, and about myself and how I was employed at good pay by the publishers of THE CALIFORNIAN to come up there and write an able criticism upon the pictures in the Art Union—indeed I concealed nothing from Brown, and in return he concealed nothing from me, but told me everything he could recollect about his rum old mother, and his grand-mother, and all his relations, in fact. And so we talked and talked, and exchanged these tender heart-reminiscences until the sun drooped far in the West, and then Brown said "Let's go down and take a drink."

MARK TWAIN.

CALIFORNIAN, *March* 18, 1865.

CHAPTER VIII

𝕴mportant 𝕮orrespondence

BETWEEN MR. MARK TWAIN OF SAN FRANCISCO, AND REV. BISHOP HAWKS, D.D., OF NEW YORK, REV. PHILLIPS BROOKS OF PHILADELPHIA, AND REV. DR. CUMMINGS OF CHICAGO, CONCERNING THE OCCUPANCY OF GRACE CATHEDRAL.

F O R a long time I have taken a deep interest in the efforts being made to induce the above-name distinguished clergymen—or, rather, some one of them—to come out here and occupy the pulpit of the noble edifice known as Grace Cathedral. And when I saw that the vestry were uniformly unsuccessful, although doing all that they possibly could to attain their object, I felt it my duty to come forward and throw the weight of my influence—such as it might be—in favor of the laudable undertaking. That by so doing I was not seeking to curry favor with the vestry—and that my actions were prompted by no selfish motive of any kind whatever—is sufficiently evidenced by the fact that I am not a member of Grace Church, and never had any conversation with the vestry upon the subject in hand, and never even hinted to them that I was going to write to the clergymen. What I have done in the matter I did of my own free will and accord, without any solicitation from anybody, and my actions were dictated solely by a spirit of enlarged charity and good feeling toward the congregation of Grace Cathedral. I seek no reward for my services; I desire none but the approval of my own conscience and the satisfaction of knowing I have done that which I conceived to be my duty, to the best of my ability.   M. T.

The correspondence which passed between myself and the Rev. Dr. Hawks was as follows:

LETTER FROM MYSELF TO BISHOP HAWKS

SAN FRANCISCO, March, 1865.

REV. DR. HAWKS—*Dear Doctor.*—Since I heard that you have telegraphed the vestry of Grace Cathedral here, that you cannot come out to San Francisco and carry on a church at the terms offered you, viz: $7,000 a year, I have concluded to write you on the subject myself. A word in your ear: say nothing to anybody—keep dark—but just pack up your traps and come along out here—I will see that it is all right. That $7,000 dodge was only a *bid*—nothing more. They never expected you to clinch a bargain like that. I will go to work and get up a little competition among the cloth, and the result of it will be that you will make more money in six months here than you would in New York in a year. I can do it. I have a great deal of influence with the clergy here, and especially with the Rev. Dr. Wadsworth and the Rev. Mr. Stebbins—I write their sermons for them. [This latter fact is not generally known, however, and maybe you had as well not mention it.] I can get them to strike for higher wages any time.

You would like this berth. It has a greater number of attractive features than any I know of. It is such a magnificent field, for one thing,—why, sinners are so thick that you can't throw out your line without hooking several of them; you'd be surprised—the flattest old sermon a man can grind out is bound to corral half a dozen. You see, you can do such a land-office business on such a small capital. Why, I wrote the most rambling, incomprehensible harangue of a sermon you ever heard in your life for one of the Episcopalian ministers here, and he landed seventeen with it at the first dash; then I trimmed it up to suit Methodist doctrine, and the Rev. Mr. Thomas got eleven more; I tinkered the doctrinal points again, and Stebbins made a lot of Unitarian converts with it; I worked it over once more, and Dr. Wadsworth did almost as well with it as he usually does with my ablest compositions. It was passed around, after that, from church to church, undergoing changes of dress as before, to suit the vicissitudes of doctrinal climate, until it went the entire rounds. During its career we took in, altogether, a hundred and eighteen of the most abject reprobates that ever traveled on the broad road to destruction.

You would find this a remarkably easy berth—one man to give out the hymns, another to do the praying, another to read the chapter from the Testament—you would have nothing in the world to do but read the litany and preach—no, not *read* the litany, but sing it. They sing the litany here, in the Pontifical Grand Mass style, which is pleasanter and more attractive than to read it. You need not mind that, though; the tune is not difficult, and required no more musical taste or education than is required to sell "Twenty-four—self-sealing —envelopes—for f-o-u-r cents," in your city. I like to hear the litany sung. Perhaps there is hardly enough variety in the music, but still the effect is very fine. Bishop Kip never could sing worth a cent, though. However, he has gone to Europe now to learn. Yes, as I said before, you would have nothing in the world to do but preach and sing that litany; and, between you and me, Doc, as regards the music, if you could manage to ring in a few of the popular and familiar old tunes that the people love so well you would be almost certain to create a sensation. I think I can safely promise you that. I am satisfied that you could do many a thing that would attract less attention than would result from adding a spirited variety to the music of the litany.

Your preaching will be easy. Bring along a barrel of your old obsolete sermons; the people here will never know the difference.

Drop me a line, Hawks; I don't know you, except by reputation, but I like you all the same. And don't you fret about the salary. I'll make *that* all right, you know. You need not mention to the vestry of Grace Cathedral, though, that I have been communicating with you on this subject. You see, I do not belong to their church, and they might think I was taking too much trouble on their account—though I assure you, upon my honor, it is no trouble in the world to me; I don't mind it; I am not busy now, and I would rather do it than not. All I want is to have a sure thing that you get your rights. You can depend upon me. I'll see you through this business as straight as a shingle; I haven't been drifting around all my life for nothing. I know a good deal more than a boiled carrot, though I may not appear to. And although I am not of the elect, so to speak, I take a strong interest in these things, nevertheless, and I am not going to stand by and see them come any seven-thousand-dollar arrangement over you. I have sent them word in your name that you won't take less than $18,000, and that you can get $25,000 in greenbacks at home. I also intimated that I was going to write your sermons—I thought it might have a good effect, and every little helps, you know. So you can just pack up and come along—it will be all right—I am satisfied of that. You needn't bring any shirts, I have got enough for us both. You will find there is nothing mean about *me*—I'll wear your clothes, and you can wear mine, just the same as so many twin brothers. When I like a man, I *like* him, and I go to my death for him. My friends will all be fond of you, and will take to you as naturally as if they had known you a century. I will introduce you, and you will be all right. You can always depend on them. If you were to point out a man and say you did not like him, they would carve him in a minute.

Hurry along, Bishop. I shall be on the lookout for you, and will take you right to my house and you can stay there as long as you like, and it shan't cost you a cent.

MARK TWAIN.

REPLY OF BISHOP HAWKS

NEW YORK, April, 1865.

MY DEAR MARK.—I had never heard of you before I received your kind letter, but I feel acquainted with you now as

if I had known you for years. I see that you understand how
it is with us poor laborers in the vineyard, and feel for us in
our struggles to gain a livelihood. You will be blessed for this
—you will have your reward for the deeds done in the flesh—
you will get your deserts hereafter. I am really sorry I cannot
visit San Francisco, for I can see now that it must be a pleasant field for the earnest worker to toil in; but it was ordered
otherwise, and I submit with becoming humility. My refusal
of the position at $7,000 a year was not precisely meant to be
final, but was intended for what the ungodly term a "flyer"
—the object being, of course, to bring about an increase of
the amount. That object was legitimate and proper, since it
so nearly affects the interests not only of myself but of those
who depend upon me for sustenance and support. Perhaps
you remember a remark made once to a vestry who had been
solicited to increase my salary, my family being a pretty large
one: they declined, and said it was promised that Providence
would take care of the young ravens. I immediately retorted,
in my happiest vein, that there was no similar promise concerning the young Hawks, though! I thought it was very
good, at the time. The recollection of it has solaced many a
weary hour since then, when all the world around me seemed
dark and cheerless, and it is a source of tranquil satisfaction
to me to think of it even at this day.

No; I hardly meant my decision to be final, as I said before,
but subsequent events have compelled that result in spite of
me. I threw up my parish in Baltimore, although it was pay-
ing me very handsomely, and came to New York to see how
things were going in our line. I have prospered beyond my
highest expectations. I selected a lot of my best sermons—old
ones that had been forgotten by everybody—and once a week
I let one of them off in the Church of the Annunciation here.
The spirit of the ancient sermons bubbled forth with a bead
on it and permeated the hearts of the congregation with a
new life, such as the worn body feels when it is refreshed with
rare old wine. It was a great hit. The timely arrival of the

"call" from San Francisco insured success to me. The people appreciated my merits at once. A number of gentlemen immediately clubbed together and offered me $10,000 a year, and agreed to purchase for me the Church of St. George the Martyr, up town, or to build a new house of worship for me if I preferred it. I closed with them on these terms, my dear Mark, for I feel that so long as not even the little sparrows are suffered to fall to the ground unnoted, I shall be mercifully cared for; and besides, I know that come what may, I can always eke out an existence so long as the cotton trade holds out as good as it is now. I am in cotton to some extent, you understand, and that is one reason why I cannot venture to leave here just at present to accept the position offered me in San Francisco. You see I have some small investments in that line which are as yet in an undecided state, and must be looked after.

But time flies, Mark, time flies; and I must bring this screed to a close and say farewell—and if forever, then forever fare thee well. But I shall never forget you, Mark—never!

Your generous solicitude in my behalf—your splendid inventive ability in conceiving of messages to the vestry calculated to make them offer me a higher salary—your sublime intrepidity in tendering those messages as having come from me—your profound sagacity in chaining and riveting the infatuation of the vestry with the intimation that you were going to write my sermons for me—your gorgeous liberality in offering to divide your shirts with me and to make common property of all other wearing apparel belonging to both parties—your cordial tender of your friends' affections and their very extraordinary services—your noble hospitality in providing a home for me in your palatial mansion—all these things call for my highest admiration and gratitude, and call not in vain, my dearest Mark. I shall never cease to pray for you and hold you in kindly and tearful remembrance. Once more, my gifted friend, accept the fervent thanks and the best wishes of   Your obliged servant,

REV. DR. HAWKS.

———

Writes a beautiful letter, don't he?

But when the Bishop uses a tabooed expression, and talks glibly about doing a certain thing "just for a flyer," don't he shoulder the responsibility of it on to "the ungodly," with a rare grace?

And what a solid comfort that execrable joke has been to his declining years, hasn't it? If he goes on thinking about it and swelling himself up on account of it, he will be wanting a salary after a while that will break any church that hires him. However, if he enjoys it, and really thinks it *was* a good joke, I am very sure I don't want to dilute his pleasure in the least by dispelling the illusion. It reminds me, though, of a neat remark which the editor of *Harper's Magazine* made three years ago, in an article wherein he was pleading for charity for the harmless vanity of poor devil scribblers who imagine they are gifted with genius. He said *they* didn't know but what their writing was fine—and then he says: "Don't poor Martin Farquhar Tupper fondle his platitudes and think they are poems?" That's it. Let the Bishop fondle his little joke—no doubt it is just as good to him as if it were the very soul of humor.

But I wonder who in the mischief *is* "St.-George-the-Martyr-Up-Town?" However, no matter—the Bishop is not going to take his chances altogether with St.-George-the-Martyr-Up-Town, or with the little sparrows that are subject to accidents, either—he has a judicious eye on cotton. And he is right, too. Nobody deserves to be helped who don't try to help himself, and "faith without works" is a risky doctrine.

Now, what is your idea about his last paragraph? Don't you think he is spreading it on rather thick?—as "the ungodly" would term it. Do you really think there is any rain behind all that thunder and lightning? Do you suppose he really means it? They are mighty powerful adjectives—uncommonly powerful adjectives—and sometimes I seem to smell a faint odor of irony about them. But that could hardly be. He evidently loves me. Why, if I could be brought to believe that that reverend old humorist was discharging any sarcasm at me, I would never write to him again as long as I live. Thinks I will "get my deserts hereafter"—I don't hardly like the ring of that, altogether.

He says he will pray for me, though. Well, he couldn't do anything that would fit my case better, and he couldn't find a subject who would thank him more kindly for it than I would. I suppose I shall come in under the head of "sinners at large"—but I don't mind that; I am no better than any other sinner and I am not entitled to especial consideration. They pray for the congregation first, you know—and with considerable vim; then they pray mildly for other denominations; then for the near relations of the congregation; then for their distant relatives; then for the surrounding community; then for the State; then for the Government officers; then for the United States; then for North America; then for the whole Continent; then for England, Ireland and Scotland; France, Germany and Italy; Russia, Prussia and Austria; then for the inhabitants of Norway, Sweden and Timbuctoo; and those of Saturn, Jupiter and New Jersey; and then they give the niggers a lift, and the Hindoos a lift, and the Turks a lift, and the Chinese a lift; and then, after they have got the fountain of mercy baled out as dry as an ash-hopper, they bespeak the sediment left in the bottom of it for us poor "sinners at large."

It ain't just exactly fair, *is* it? Sometimes, (being a sort of a Presbyterian in a general way, and a brevet member of one of the principal churches of that denomination,) I stand up in devout attitude, with downcast eyes, and hands clasped upon the back of the pew before me, and listen attentively and ex-

pectantly for awhile; and then rest upon one foot for a
season; and then upon the other; and then insert my hands
under my coat-tails and stand erect and look solemn; and
then fold my arms and droop forward and look dejected; and
then cast my eye furtively at the minister; and then at the
congregation; and then grow absent-minded, and catch myself counting the lace bonnets; and marking the drowsy members; and noting the wide-awake ones; and averaging the bald
heads; and afterwards descend to indolent conjectures as to
whether the buzzing fly that keeps stumbling up the window-
pane and sliding down backwards again will ever accomplish
his object to his satisfaction; and, finally, I give up and re-
lapse into a dreary reverie—and about this time the minister
reaches my department, and brings me back to hope and consciousness with a kind word for the poor "sinners at large."

Sometimes we are even forgotten altogether and left out in
the cold—and then I call to mind the vulgar little boy who
was fond of hot biscuits, and whose mother promised him that
he should have all that were left if he would stay away and
keep quiet and be a good little boy while the strange guest
ate his breakfast; and who watched that voracious guest till
the growing apprehension in his young bosom gave place to
demonstrated ruin and then sung out: "There! I know'd how
it was goin' to be—I know'd how it was goin' to be, from the
start! Blamed if he hain't gobbled the last biscuit!"

I do not complain, though, because it is very seldom that
the Hindoos and the Turks and the Chinese get all the aton-
ing biscuits and leave us sinners at large to go hungry. They
do remain at the board a long time, though, and we often get
a little tired waiting for our turn. How would it do to be less
diffuse? How would it do to ask a blessing upon the speciali-
ties—I mean the congregation and the immediate community—and then include the whole broad universe in one glowing fervent appeal? How would it answer to adopt the simplicity and the beauty and the brevity and the comprehen-

siveness of the Lord's Prayer as a model? But perhaps I am wandering out of my jurisdiction.

The letters I wrote to the Rev. Phillips Brooks of Philadelphia, and the Rev. Dr. Cummings of Chicago, urging them to come here and take charge of Grace Cathedral, and offering them my countenance and support, will be published next week, together with their replies to the same.

MARK TWAIN.

CALIFORNIAN, *May* 6, 1865.

CHAPTER IX

Further of Mr. Mark Twain's Important Correspondence

I PROMISED, last week, that I would publish in the present number of THE CALIFORNIAN the correspondence held between myself and Rev. Phillips Brooks of Philadelphia, and Rev. Dr. Cummings of Chicago, but I must now beg you to release me from that promise. I have just received telegrams from these distinguished clergymen suggesting the impolicy of printing their letters; the suggestion is accompanied by arguments, so able, so pointed and so conclusive that, although I saw no impropriety in it before, I am forced now to concede that it *would* be very impolitic to publish their letters. It could do but little good, perhaps, and might really do harm, in awakening a diseased curiosity in the public mind concerning the private matters of ministers of the gospel. The telegrams and accompanying arguments are as follows:

FROM REV. PHILLIPS BROOKS

PHILADELPHIA, Friday, May 12.

MR. MICK TWINE:* Am told you have published Bishop Hawks' letter. You'll ruin the clergy! Don't—*don't* publish mine. Listen to reason—come, now, don't make an ass of yourself. Draw on me for five hundred dollars.

REV. PHILLIPS BROOKS.

[Although I feel it my duty to suppress his letter, it is proper to state for the information of the public, that Phil.

gets a higher salary where he is, and consequently he cannot come out here and take charge of Grace Cathedral. *Mem.*— He is in petroleum to some extent, also.—M. T.]

FROM REV. DR. CUMMINGS

CHICAGO, Thursday, May 11.

MR. MACSWAIN:* Have you really been stupid enough to publish Bishop Hawks' letter? Ge-whillikins! don't publish mine. Don't be a fool, Mike.* Draw on me for five or six hundred.   REV. DR.'CUMMINGS.

[I am conscious that it would be improper to print the Doctor's letter, but it may be as well to observe that *he* also gets a higher salary where he is, and consequently he cannot come out here and take charge of Grace Cathedral. *Mem.*— He is speculating a little in grain.—M. T.]

I am afraid I was rather hasty in publishing Bishop Hawks' letter. I am sorry I did it. I suppose there is no chance now to get an Argument out of him, this late in the day.

FOREIGN CORRESPONDENCE

I am a suffering victim of my infernal disposition to be always trying to oblige somebody without being asked to do it. Nobody asked me to help the vestry of Grace Cathedral to hire a minister; I dashed into it on my own hook, in a spirit of absurd enthusiasm, and a nice mess I have made of it. I have not succeeded in securing either of the three clergymen I wanted, but that is not the worst of it—I have brought such a swarm of low-priced back-country preachers about my ears that I begin to be a little appalled at the work of my own hands. I am afraid I have evoked a spirit that I cannot lay. A single specimen of the forty-eight letters addressed to me from the interior will suffice to show the interest my late publication has excited:

----

* Excuse the unhappy telegraph—it never spells names right.—M. T.

FROM REV. MR. BROWN

GRASSHOPPER CHATEAU, 1865.

BRO. TWAIN: I feel that the opportunity has arrived at last for me to make a return somewhat in kind for the countless blessings which have been poured—poured, as it were—upon my unworthy head. If you get the vacancy in Grace Cathedral for me, I will accept it at once, and at any price, notwithstanding I should sacrifice so much here in a worldly point of view, and entail so much unhappiness upon my loving flock by so doing—for I feel that I am "called," and it is not for me, an humble instrument, to disobey. [The splotch you observe here is a tear.] It stirs the deepest emotions in my breast to think that I shall soon leave my beloved flock: bear with this seeming childishness, my friend, for I have reared this dear flock, and tended it for years, and I fed it with spiritual food, and sheared it—ah, me, and sheared it—I cannot go on—the subject is too harrowing. But I'll take that berth for less than any man on the continent, if you'll get it for me. I send you specimen sermons—some original and some selected and worked over.   *   *   *

Your humble and obedient servant,

T. ST. MATTHEW BROWN.

——

They all want the berth at Grace Cathedral. They would all be perfectly satisfied with $7,000 a year. They are all willing to sacrifice their dearest worldly interests and break the tenderest ties that bind them to their rural homes, to come and fight the good fight in our stately church. They all feel that they could do more good and serve their master better in a wider sphere of action. They all feel stirring within them souls too vast for confinement in narrow flats and gulches. And they all want to come here and spread. And worse than all, they all devil *me* with their bosh, and send *me* their sermons to read, and come and dump their baggage in *my* hall, and take possession of *my* bed-rooms by assault, and carry *my* dinner-table by storm, instead of inflicting these miseries upon the vestry of Grace Cathedral, who are the proper victims, by virtue of their office. Why in thunder do they come harrassing *me?* What have *I* got to do with the matter? Why, I do not even belong to the church, and have got no more to do with hiring pastors for it than the Dey of Algiers has. I wish they would ease up a little on me; I mixed into this business a little too brashly—so to speak—and without due reflection; but if I get out of it once all right, I'll not mix in any more; now that's honest—I never will.

I have numerous servants, but they are all worked down. My housekeeper is on the verge of open rebellion. Yesterday she said: "I lay I'll take and hyste some of them preachers out of this mighty soon, now." And she'll do it. I shall regret it. I could entertain no sentiment but that of regret to see a clergyman "hysted" out of my establishment, but what am I to do? I cannot help it. If I were to interfere I should get "hysted" myself.

My clerical guests are healthy. Their appetites are good. They are not particular as to food. They worry along very well on spring chickens. I don't feel safe with them, though, because if it is considered that a steamboat on the Mississippi is inviting disaster when she ventures to carry more than two ministers at a time, isn't it likely that the dozen I have got in my house will eventually produce an earthquake? The tradition goes that three clergymen on a steamboat will ground her, four will sink her, and five and a gray mare added will blow her up. If I had a gray mare in my stable, I would leave this city before night.   MARK TWAIN.

CALIFORNIAN, *May* 13, 1865.

CHAPTER X

𝕿𝖍𝖊 𝕱𝖆𝖈𝖙𝖘

CONCERNING THE RECENT TROUBLE BETWEEN MR. MARK TWAIN AND MR. JOHN WILLIAM SKAE OF VIRGINIA CITY—WHEREIN IT IS ATTEMPTED TO BE PROVED THAT THE FORMER WAS NOT TO BLAME IN THE MATTER.

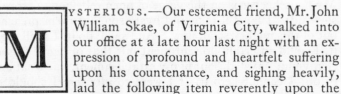 YSTERIOUS.—Our esteemed friend, Mr. John William Skae, of Virginia City, walked into our office at a late hour last night with an expression of profound and heartfelt suffering upon his countenance, and sighing heavily, laid the following item reverently upon the desk and walked slowly out again. He paused a moment at the door and seemed struggling to command his feelings sufficiently to enable him to speak, and then, nodding his head toward his manuscript, ejaculated in a broken voice, "Friend of mine—Oh how sad!" and burst into tears. We were so moved at his distress that we did not think to call him back and endeavor to comfort him until he was gone and it was too late. Our paper had already gone to press, but knowing that our friend would consider the publication of this item important, and cherishing the hope that to print it would afford a melancholy satisfaction to his sorrowing heart, we stopped the press at once and inserted it in our columns:

Distressing Accident—Last evening about 6 o'clock, as Mr. William Schuyler, an old and respectable citizen of South Park, was leaving his residence to go down town, as has been his usual custom for many years, with the exception only of a short interval in the Spring of 1850 during which he was confined to his bed by injuries received in attempting to stop a runaway horse by thoughtlessly placing himself directly in its wake and throwing up his hands and shouting, which, if he had done so even a single moment sooner must inevitably have frightened the animal still more instead of checking its speed, although disastrous enough to himself, as it was and rendered more melancholy and distressing by reason of the presence of his wife's mother, who was there and saw the sad occurrence, notwithstanding it is at least likely, though not necessarily so, that she should be reconnoitering in another direction when incidents occur, not being vivacious and on the lookout, as a general thing, but even the reverse, as her own mother is said to have stated, who is no more, but died in the full hope of a glorious resurrection, upwards of three years ago, aged 86, being 'a Christian woman and without guile, as it were, or property, in consequence of the fire of 1849, which destroyed every blasted thing she had in the world. But such is life. Let us all take warning by this solemn occurrence, and let us endeavor so to conduct ourselves that when we come to die we can do it. Let us place our hands upon our hearts and say with earnestness and sincerity that from this day forth we will beware of the intoxicating bowl.—*First Edition of the Californian.*

————

(SECOND EDITION OF THE CALIFORNIAN)

The boss editor has been in here raising the very mischief, and tearing his hair and kicking the furniture about, and abusing me like a pick-pocket. He says that every time he leaves me in charge of the paper for half an hour I get imposed upon by the first infant or the first idiot that comes along. And he says that distressing item of Johnny Skae's is nothing but a lot of distressing bosh, and has got no point to it, and no sense in it, and no information in it, and that there was no earthly necessity for stopping the press to publish it. He says every man he meets has insinuated that somebody about THE CALIFORNIAN office has gone crazy.

Now all this comes of being good-hearted. If I had been as unaccommodating and unsympathetic as some people, I would have told Johnny Skae that I wouldn't receive his communication at such a late hour, and to go to blazes with it—but no, his snuffling distress touched my heart, and I jumped at the chance of doing something to modify his misery. I never read his item to see whether there was anything wrong about it, but hastily wrote the few lines which preceded it and sent it to the printers. And what has my kindness done for me? It has done nothing but bring down upon me a storm of abuse and ornamental blasphemy.

Now I will just read that item myself, and see if there is any foundation for all this fuss. And if there is, the author of it shall hear from me.

*   *   *   *   *   *   *

I have read it, and I am bound to admit that it seems a little mixed at a first glance. However, I will peruse it once more.

*   *   *   *   *   *   *

I have read it again, and it does really seem a good deal more mixed than ever.

*   *   *   *   *   *   *

I have read it over five times, but if I can get at the meaning of it, I wish I may get my just deserts. It won't bear analysis. There are things about it which I cannot understand at all. It don't say what ever became of William Schuyler. It just says enough about him to get one interested in his career, and then drops him. Who is William Schuyler, anyhow, and what part of South Park did he live in? and if he started down town at six o'clock, did he ever get there? and if he did, did anything happen to him? is *he* the individual that met with the "distressing accident?" Considering the elaborate circumstantiality of detail observable in the item, it seems to me that it ought to contain more information than it does. On the contrary, it is obscure—and not only obscure but utterly incomprehensible. Was the breaking of Mr. Schuyler's leg fifteen years ago the "distressing accident" that plunged Mr. Skae into unspeakable grief, and caused him to come up here at dead of night and stop our press to acquaint the world with the unfortunate circumstance? Or did the "distressing accident" consist in the destruction of Schuyler's mother-in-law's property in early times? or did it consist in the death of that person herself three years ago, (albeit it does not appear that she died by accident?) In a word, what *did* that "distressing accident" consist in? What did that driveling ass of a Schuyler stand *in the wake* of a runaway horse for, with his shouting and gesticulating, if he wanted to stop him? And how the mischief could he get run over by a horse that had already passed beyond him? And what are we to "take warning" by? and how is this extraordinary chapter of incomprehensibilities going to be a "lesson" to us? And above all, what has the "intoxicating bowl" got to do with it, anyhow? It is not stated that Schuyler drank, or that his wife drank, or that his mother-in-law drank, or that the horse drank—wherefore, then, the reference to the intoxicating bowl? It does seem to me that if Mr. Skae had let the intoxicating bowl alone himself, he never would have got into so much trouble about this infernal imaginary distressing accident. I have read his absurd item over and over again, with all its insinuating plausibility, until my head swims, but I can make neither head nor tail of it. There certainly seems to have been an accident of some kind or other, but it is impossible to determine what the nature of it was, or who was the sufferer by it. I do not like to do it, but I feel compelled to request that the next time anything happens to one of Mr. Skae's friends, he will append such explanatory notes to his account of it as will enable me to find out what sort of an accident it was and who it happened to. I had rather all his friends should die than that I should be driven to the verge of lunacy again in trying to cipher out the meaning of another such production as the above.

But not, after all this fuss that has been made by the chief cook about this item, I do not see that it is any more obscure than the general run of local items in the daily papers after all. You don't usually find out much by reading local items, and you don't in the case of Johnny Skae's item. But it is just THE CALIFORNIAN's style to be so disgustingly particular and so distressingly hypercritical. If Stiggers throws off one of his graceful little jokes, ten to one THE CALIFORNIAN will come out the very next Saturday and find fault with it, be-

cause there ain't any point to it—find fault with it because
there is no place in it where you can laugh—find fault with it
because a man feels humiliated after reading it. They don't
appear to know how to discriminate. They don't appear to
understand that there are different kinds of jokes, and that
Stiggers' jokes may be of that kind. No; they give a man no
credit for originality—for striking out into new paths and
opening up new domains of humor; they overlook all that,
and just cramp an *Alta* joke down to their own narrow and
illiberal notion of what a joke ought to be, and then if they
find it hasn't got any point to it, they turn up their noses and
say it isn't any joke at all. I do despise such meanness.

And they are just the same way with the *Flag's* poetry.
They never stop to reflect that the author may be striking out
into new fields of poetry—no; they simply say, "Stuff! this
poem's got no sense in it; and it hasn't got any rhyme to it to
speak of; and there is no more rhythm about it than there is
to a Chinese oration"—and then, just on this evidence alone,
they presume to say it's not poetry at all.

And so with the *Call's* grammar. If the local of the *Call* gets
to branching out into new and aggravating combinations of
words and phrases, they don't stop to think that maybe he is
humbly trying to start something fresh in English composition and thus make his productions more curious and entertaining—not they; they just bite into him at once, and say he
isn't writing grammar. And why? We repeat: And why? Why,
merely because he don't choose to be the slave of their notions
and Murray's.

And just so with the *Bulletin's* country correspondent.
Because one of those mild and unoffending dry-goods clerks
with his hair parted in the middle writes down to the *Bulletin*
in a column and a half how he took the stage for Calistoga;
and paid his fare; and got his change; stating the amount of
the same; and that he had thought it would be more; but un-
pretentiously intimates that it could be a matter of no consequence to him one way or the other; and then goes on to tell

about who he found at the Springs; and who he treated; and
who treated him; and proceeds to give the initials of all the
ladies of quality sojourning there; and does it in such a way
as to conceal, as far as possible, how much they dote on his
society; and then tells how he took a bath; and how the soap
escaped from his fingers; and describes with infinite humor
the splashing and scrambling he had to go through with before he got it again; and tells how he took a breezy gallop in
the early morning at 9 A. M. with Gen. E. B. G.'s charming
and accomplished daughter, and how the two, with souls
o'ercharged with emotions too deep for utterance, beheld the
glorious sun bathing the eastern hills with the brilliant mag-
nificence of his truly gorgeous splendor, thus recalling to them
tearful reminiscences of other scenes and other climes, when
their hearts were young and as yet unseared by the cold
clammy hand of the vain, heartless world—dreaming thus, in
blissful unconsciousness, he of the stream of ants travelling up
his body and down the back of his neck, and she of the galli-
nipper sucking the tip-end of her nose—because one of these
inoffensive pleasure-going correspondents writes all this to
the *Bulletin*, I say, THE CALIFORNIAN gets irritated and acri-
monious in a moment, and says it is the vilest bosh in the
world; and says there is nothing important about it, and
wonders who in the nation cares if that fellow *did* ride in the
stage, and pay his fare, and take a bath, and see the sun rise
up and slobber over the eastern hills four hours after day-
light; and asks with withering scorn, "Well, what does it all
amount to?" and wants to know who is any wiser now than
he was before he read the long-winded correspondence; and
intimates that the *Bulletin* had better be minding the commercial interests of the land than afflicting the public with
such wishy-washy trash. That is just the style of THE CALI-
FORNIAN. No correspondence is good enough for its hypercritical notions unless it has got something in it. THE CALI-
FORNIAN sharps don't stop to consider that maybe that dis-
banded clerk was up to something—that maybe he was sift-

ing around after some new realm or other in literature—that maybe perhaps he was trying to get something through his head—well, they don't stop to consider anything; they just say, because it is trivial, and awkwardly written, and stupid, and devoid of information, that it is Bosh, and that is the end of it! THE CALIFORNIAN hates originality—that is the whole thing in a nutshell. *They* know it all. They are the *only* authority—and if *they* don't like a thing, why of course it won't do. Certainly not. Now who but THE CALIFORNIAN would ever have found fault with Johnny Skae's item. No daily paper in town would, anyhow. It is after the same style, and is just as good, and as interesting and as luminous as the articles published every day in the city papers. It has got all the virtues that distinguish those articles and render them so acceptable to the public. It is not obtrusively pointed, and in this it resembles the jokes of Stiggers; it warbles smoothly and easily along, without rhyme or rhythm or reason, like the *Flag's* poetry; the eccentricity of its construction is appalling to the grammatical student, and in this it rivals the happiest achievements of the *Call;* it furnishes the most laborious and elaborate details to the eye without transmitting any information whatever to the understanding, and in this respect it will bear comparison with the most notable specimens of the *Bulletin's* country correspondence; and finally, the mysterious obscurity that curtains its general intent and meaning could not be surpassed by all the newspapers in town put together.

———

(THIRD EDITION OF THE CALIFORNIAN)

More trouble. The chief hair-splitter has been in here again raising a dust. It appears that Skae's item has disseminated the conviction that there has been a distressing accident somewhere, of some kind or other, and the people are exasperated at the agonizing uncertainty of the thing. Some have it that the accident happened to Schuyler; others say that inasmuch as Schuyler disappeared in the first clause of the item, it must have been the horse; again, others say that inasmuch as the horse disappeared in the second clause without having up to that time sustained any damage, it must have been Schuyler's wife; but others say that inasmuch as she disappeared in the third clause all right and was never mentioned again, it must have been the old woman, Schuyler's mother-in-law; still others say that inasmuch as the old woman died three years ago, and not necessarily by accident, it is too late in the day to mention it now, and so it must have been the house; but others sneer at the latter idea, and say if the burning of the house sixteen years ago was so "distressing" to Schuyler, why didn't he wait fifty years longer before publishing the incident, and then maybe he could bear it easier. But there is trouble abroad, at any rate. People are satisfied that there has been an accident, and they are furious because they cannot find out who it has happened to. They are ridiculously unreasonable. They say they don't know who Schuyler is, but that's neither here nor there—if anything has happened to him they are going to know all about it or somebody has got to suffer.

That is just what it has come to—personal violence. And it is all bred out of that snivelling lunatic's coming in here at midnight, and enlisting my sympathies with his infamous imaginary misfortune, and making me publish his woolgathering nonsense. But this is throwing away time. Something has got to be done. There has got to be an accident in the Schuyler family, and that without any unnecessary delay. Nothing else will satisfy the public. I don't know any man by the name of Schuyler, but I will go out and hunt for one. All I want now is a Schuyler. And I am bound to have a Schuyler if I have to take Schuyler Colfax. If I can only get hold of a Schuyler, I will take care of the balance of the programme—I will see that an accident happens to him as soon as possible. And failing this, I will try and furnish a disaster to the stricken Skae.   MARK TWAIN.

CALIFORNIAN, *August* 26, 1865.

CHAPTER XI

Real Estate versus Imaginary Possessions, Poetically Considered

MY KINGDOM

I HAVE a kingdom of unknown extent,
    Treasures great, its wealth without compare;
And all the pleasures men in pride invent
    Are not like mine, so free from pain and care.

'Tis all my own: no hostile power may rise
    To force me outward from its rich domain;
It hath a strength that time itself defies,
    And all invaders must assail in vain.

'Tis true sometimes its sky is overcast,
    And troublous clouds obscure the peaceful light;
Yet these are transient and so quickly past
    Its radiance seems to glow more clear and bright.

It hath a queen—my queen—whose loving reign
    No daring subject ever may dispute;
Her will is mine, and all my toil her gain,
    And when she speaks my heart with love is mute.

She sits beside me, and her gentle hand
    Guides all my hopes in this estate below;
The joys of life, the products of the land,
    Beneath her smiles in ceaseless pleasures flow.

My heart, her subject, throbs beneath her eyes,
    And sends its tides full with unbounded love,
As ocean's waters swell beneath the skies
    Drawn by the placid moon that rolls above.

What king or ruler hath a state like mine,
    That death or time can never rend apart,
Where hopes and pleasures are almost divine?
    Yet all this kingdom—One True Woman's Heart.

—[*Evening Bulletin.*]   PAUL DUOIR.

Oh, stuff! Is that all? I like your poetry, Mr. D., but I
don't "admire" to see a man raise such a thundering smoke
on such a very small capital of fire. I may be a little irritated,
because you fooled me, D., you fooled me badly. I read your
ramifications—I choose the word, D., simply because it has
five syllables, and I desire to flatter you up a little before I
abuse you; I don't know the meaning of it myself—I noticed
your grandiloquent heading, "My Kingdom," and it woke
me up; so I commenced reading your Ramifications with
avidity, and I said to myself, with my usual vulgarity, "Now
here's a man that's got a good thing." I read along, and read
along, thinking sure you were going to turn out to be King of
New Jersey, or King of the Sandwich Islands, or the lucky
monarch of a still more important kingdom, maybe—but how
my spirits fell when I came to your cheap climax! And so your
wonderful kingdom is—"A True Woman's Heart!"—with
capital letters to it! Oh, my! Now what do you want to go and
make all that row about such a thing as that for, and fool
people? Why, you put on as many frills, and make as much
fuss about your obscure "kingdom" as if it were a magnificent
institution—a first-class power among the nations—and contained a population of forty million souls, (and maybe it does,
for all you know—most kingdoms of that kind are pretty

well tenanted, my innocent royal friend.) And what does your majesty suppose you can do with your extraordinary "kingdom?" You can't sell it; you can't hire it out; you can't raise money on it. Bah! You ought to be more practical. You can keep your boasted "kingdom," since it appears to be such a comfort to you; don't come around trying to trade with me— I am very well content with

MY RANCH

I HAVE a ranch of quite unknown extent,
　　Its turnips great, its oats without compare;
And all the ranches other men may rent
　　And not like mine—so not a dern* I care

'Tis all my own—no turnstile power may rise
　　To keep me outward from its rich domain;
It hath a fence that time itself defies,
　　And all invaders must climb out again.

'Tis true sometimes with stones 'tis overcast,
　　And troublous clods offend the sens'tive sight;
Yet from the furrows I these so quickly blast,
　　Their radiant seams do show more clear and bright.

It hath a sow—*my* sow—whose love for grain
　　No swearing subject will dispute;
Her swill is mine, and all my slops her gain,
　　And when she squeaks my heart with love is mute.

[Here the machine "let down."]　　　　MARK TWAIN.

---

* This imprecation is a favorite one out in the ranching districts, and is generally used in the society of ladies, where only mild forms of expression may be indulged in.

CALIFORNIAN, *October 28, 1865.*

CHAPTER XII

"Mark Twain" Overpowered

HE *Enterprise*, having recently published one of those "affecting incidents," which are occasionally met with by "localitems," when there is a dearth of fires, runaways, etc., "Mark Twain" issues the following as a companion-piece:

UNCLE LIGE

I will now relate an affecting incident of my meeting with Uncle Lige, as a companion novelette to the one published by Dan the other day, entitled "Uncle Henry."

A day of two since—before the late stormy weather—I was taking a quiet stroll in the western suburbs of the city. The day was sunny and pleasant. In front of a small but neat "bit house," seated upon a bank—a worn out and discarded faro bank—I saw a man and a little girl. The sight was too much for me, and I burst into tears. Oh, God! I cried, this is too rough! After the violence of my emotion had in a manner spent itself, I ventured to look once more upon that touching picture. The left hand of the girl (how well I recollect which hand it was! by the warts on it)—a fair-haired, sweet-faced child of about eight years of age—rested upon the right shoulder (how perfectly I remember it was his right shoulder, because his left shoulder had been sawed off in a saw-mill) of the man by whose side she was seated. She was gazing toward the summit of Lone Mountain, and prating of the gravestones on the top of it and of the sunshine and Diggers resting on its tomb-clad slopes. The head of the man drooped forward till his face almost rested upon his breast, and he seemed intently listening. It was only a pleasing pretence, though, for there was nothing for him to hear save the rattling of the carriages on the gravel road beside him, and he could have straightened himself up and heard that easy enough, poor fellow. As I approached, the child observed me, notwithstanding her extreme youth, and ceasing to talk, smilingly looked at me, strange as it may seem. I stopped, again almost overpowered, but after a struggle I mastered my feelings sufficiently to proceed. I gave her a smile—or rather, I swapped her one in return for the one I had just received, and she said:

"This is Uncle Lige—poor blind-drunk Uncle Lige."

This burst of confidence from an entire stranger, and one so young withal, caused my subjugated emotions to surge up in my breast once more, but again, with a strong effort, I controlled them. I looked at the wine-bred cauliflower on the poor man's nose and saw how it had all happened.

"Yes," said he, noticing by my eloquent countenance that I *had* seen how it had all happened, notwithstanding nothing had been said yet about anything having happened, "Yes, it happened in Reeseriv' a year ago; since tha(ic)at time been living here with broth—Robert'n lill Addie (*e ick!*)."

"Oh, he's the best uncle, and tells me such stories!" cried the little girl.

"At's aw-ri, you know (ick!)—at's aw-ri," said the kind-hearted, gentle old man, spitting on his shirt bosom and slurring it off with his hand.

The child leaned quickly forward and kissed his poor blossomy face. We beheld two great tears start from the man's sightless eyes, but when they saw what sort of country they had got to travel over, they went back again. Kissing the child again and again and once more and then several times, and afterwards repeating it, he said:

"H(o-ook!)—oorah for Melical eagle star-spalgle baller!

At's aw-ri, you know—(ick!)—at's aw-ri"—and he stroked her sunny curls and spit on his shirt bosom again.

This affecting scene was too much for my already overcharged feelings, and I burst into a flood of tears and hurried from the spot.

Such is the touching story of Uncle Lige. It may not be quite as sick as Dan's, but there is every bit as much reasonable material in it for a big calk like either of us to cry over. Cannot you publish the two novelettes in book form and send them forth to destroy such of our fellow citizens as are spared by the cholera?

CALIFORNIAN, *December 2*, 1865.

CHAPTER XIII

𝕿𝖍𝖊 𝕮𝖊𝖑𝖊𝖇𝖗𝖆𝖙𝖊𝖉 𝕵𝖚𝖒𝖕𝖎𝖓𝖌 𝕱𝖗𝖔𝖌 𝖔𝖋 𝕮𝖆𝖑𝖆𝖛𝖊𝖗𝖆𝖘 𝕮𝖔𝖚𝖓𝖙𝖞

BY MARK TWAIN

[THE *Saturday Press* introduces this sketch in the following complimentary manner: "We give up the principal portion of our editorial space to-day, to an exquisitely humorous sketch—'Jim and his Jumping Frog'—by Mark Twain, who will shortly become a regular contributor to our columns. Mark Twain is the assumed name of a writer in California who has long been a favorite contributor to the San Francisco press, from which his articles have been so extensively copied as to make him nearly as well known as Artemus Ward."]

M R. A. WARD—DEAR SIR: Well, I called on good-natured, garrulous old Simon Wheeler, and I inquired after your friend Leonidas W. Greeley, as you requested me to do, and I hereunto append the result. If you can get any information out of it you are cordially welcome to it. I have a lurking suspicion that your Leonidas W. Greeley is a myth—that you never knew such a personage, and that you only conjectured that if I asked old Wheeler about him it would remind him of his infamous *Jim* Greeley, and he would go to work and bore me nearly to death with some infernal reminiscence of him as long and tedious as it should be useless to me. If that was your design, Mr. Ward, it will gratify you to know that it succeeded.

I found Simon Wheeler dozing comfortably by the bar-room stove of the old dilapidated tavern in the ancient mining

I am reprinting the original version which differs from the familiar one which has Smiley instead of Greeley.—EDITOR.

camp at Angel's, and I noticed that he was fat and bald-headed, and had an expression of winning gentleness and simplicity upon his tranquil countenance. He roused up and gave me good-day. I told him a friend of mine had commissioned me to make some inquiries about a cherished companion of his boyhood named Leonidas W. Greeley—Rev. Leonidas W. Greeley—a young minister of the Gospel, who he had heard was at one time a resident of Angel's Camp. I added that if Mr. Wheeler could tell me anything about this Rev. Leonidas W. Greeley, I would feel under many obligations to him.

Simon Wheeler backed me into a corner and blockaded me there with his chair—and then sat me down and reeled off the monotonous narrative which follows this paragraph. He never smiled, he never frowned, he never changed his voice from the gentle-flowing key to which he turned the initial sentence, he never betrayed the slightest suspicion of enthusiasm—but all through the interminable narrative there ran a vein of impressive earnestness and sincerity, which showed me plainly that so far from his imagining that there was anything ridiculous or funny about his story, he regarded it as a really important matter, and admired its two heroes as men of transcendent genius in *finesse*. To me, the spectacle of a man drifting serenely along through such a queer yarn without ever smiling was exquisitely absurd. As I said before, I asked him to tell me what he knew of Rev. Leonidas W. Greeley, and he replied as follows. I let him go on in his own way, and never interrupted him once:

There was a feller here once by the name of *Jim* Greeley, in the winter of '49—or maybe it was the spring of '50—I don't recollect exactly, some how, though what makes me think it was one or the other is because I remember the big flume wasn't finished when he first come to the camp; but anyway, he was the curiosest man about always betting on anything that turned up you ever see, if he could get anybody to bet on the other side, and if he couldn't he'd change sides—any way that suited the other man would suit *him*—any way just so's he got a bet, *he* was satisfied. But still, he was lucky—uncommon lucky; he most always come out winner. He was always ready and laying for a chance; there couldn't be no solitry thing mentioned but that feller'd offer to bet on it—and take any side you please, as I was just telling you: if there was a horse race, you'd find him flush or you find him busted at the end of it; if there was a dog-fight, he'd bet on it; if there was a cat-fight, he'd bet on it; if there was a chicken-fight, he'd bet on it; why if there was two birds sitting on a fence, he would bet you which one would fly first—or if there was a camp-meeting he would be there reglar to bet on Parson Walker, which he judged to be the best exhorter about here, and so he was, too, and a good man; if he even see a straddle-bug start to go any wheres, he would bet you how long it would take him to get wherever he was going to, and if you took him up he would foller that straddle-bug to Mexico but what he would find out where he was bound for and how long he was on the road. Lots of the boys here has seen that Greeley and can tell you about him. Why, it never made no difference to *him*—he would bet on *anything*—the dangdest feller. Parson Walker's wife laid very sick, once, for a good while, and it seemed as if they warn't going to save her; but one morning he come in and Greeley asked how she was, and he said she was considerable better—thank the Lord for his inf'nit mercy—and coming on so smart that with the blessing of Providence she'd get well yet—and Greeley, before he thought, says: "Well, I'll resk two-and-a-half that she don't, anyway."

Thish-yer Greeley had a mare—the boys called her the fifteen-minute nag, but that was only in fun, you know, because, of course, she was faster than that—and he used to win money on that horse, for all she was so slow and always had the asthma, or the distemper, or the consumption, or something of that kind. They used to give her two or three hundred yards' start, and then pass her under way; but al-

ways at the fag-end of the race she'd get excited and desperate like, and come cavorting and spraddling up, and scatter-
ing her legs around limber, sometimes in the air, and sometimes out to one side amongst the fences, and kicking up
m-o-r-e dust, and raising m-o-r-e racket with her coughing
and sneezing and blowing her nose—and always fetch up at
the stand just about a neck ahead, as near as you could
cipher it down.

And he had a little small bull pup, that to look at him you'd
think he warn't worth a cent, but to set around and look
onery, and lay for a chance to steal something. But as soon as
money was up on him he was a different dog—his under-
jaw'd begin to stick out like the for'castle of a steamboat, and
his teeth would uncover, and shine savage like the furnaces.
And a dog might tackle him, and bully-rag him, and bite him,
and throw him over his shoulder two or three times, and
Andrew Jackson—which was the name of the pup—Andrew
Jackson would never let on but what he was satisfied, and
hadn't expected nothing else—and the bets being doubled
and doubled on the other side all the time, till the money was
all up—and then all of a sudden he would grab that other dog
just by the joint of his hind leg and freeze to it—not chaw,
you understand, but only just grip and hang on till they
throwed up the sponge, if it was a year. Greeley always came
out winner on that pup till he harnessed a dog once that
didn't have no hind legs, because they'd been sawed off in a
circular saw, and when the thing had gone along far enough,
and the money was all up, and he come to make a snatch for
his pet holt, he saw in a minute how he'd been imposed on,
and how the other dog had him in the door, so to speak, and
he 'peared surprised, and then he looked sorter discouraged
like, and didn't try no more to win the fight, and so he got
shucked out bad. He give Greeley a look as much as to say
his heart was broke, and it was *his* fault, for putting up a dog
that hadn't no hind legs for him to take holt of, which was his
main dependence in a fight, and then he limped off a piece,

and laid down and died. It was a good pup, was that Andrew Jackson, and would have made a name for hisself if he'd lived, for the stuff was in him, and he had genius—I know it, because he hadn't had no opportunities to speak of, and it don't stand to reason that a dog could make such a fight as he could under them circumstances, if he hadn't no talent. It always makes me feel sorry when I think of that last fight of his'n, and the way it turned out.

Well, thish-yer Greeley had rat-tarriers and chicken cocks, and tom-cats, and all them kind of things, till you couldn't rest, and you couldn't fetch nothing for him to bet on but he'd match you. He ketched a frog one day and took him home and said he cal'lated to educate him; and so he never done nothing for three months but set in his back yard and learn that frog to jump. And you bet you he *did* learn him, too. He'd give him a little punch behind, and the next minute you'd see that frog whirling in the air like a doughnut—see him turn one summerset, or maybe a couple, if he got a good start, and come down flat-footed and all right, like a cat. He got him up so in the matter of catching flies, and kept him in practice so constant, that he'd nail a fly every time as far as he could see him. Greeley said all a frog wanted was education, and he could do most anything—and I believe him. Why, I've seen him send Dan'l Webster down here on this floor—Dan'l Webster was the name of the frog—and sing out "Flies! Dan'l, flies," quicker'n you could wink, he'd spring straight up, and snake a fly off'n the counter there, and flop down on the floor again as solid as a gob of mud, and fall to scratching the side of his head with his hind foot as indifferent as if he hadn't no idea he'd done any more'n any frog might do. You never see a frog so modest and straightfor'ard as he was, for all he was so gifted. And when it come to fair-and-square jumping on a dead level, he could get over more ground at one straddle than any animal of his breed you ever see. Jumping on a dead level was his strong suit, you understand, and when it come to that, Greeley would ante up money on him as long as he had a red. Greeley was monstrous proud of his frog, and well he might be, for fellers that had travelled and been everywheres, all said he laid over any frog that ever *they* see.

Well, Greeley kept the beast in a little lattice box, and he used to fetch him down town sometimes and lay for a bet. One day a feller—a stranger in the camp, he was—come across him with his box, and says:

"What might it be that you've got in the box?"

And Greeley says, sorter indifferent like, "It might be a parrot, or it might be a canary, maybe, but it ain't—it's only just a frog."

And the feller took it, and looked at it careful, and turned it round this way and that, and says, "H'm—so 'tis. Well, what's *he* good for?"

"Well," Greeley says, easy and careless, "He's good enough for *one* thing I should judge—he can out-jump ary frog in Calaveras county."

The feller took the box again, and took another long, particular look, and give it back to Greeley and says, very deliberate, "Well—I don't see no points about that frog that's any better'n any other frog."

"Maybe you don't," Greeley says. "Maybe you understand frogs, and maybe you don't understand 'em; maybe you've had experience, and maybe you ain't only a amature, as it were. Anyways, I've got *my* opinion, and I'll resk forty dollars that he can outjump ary frog in Calaveras county."

And the feller studied a minute, and then says, kinder sad, like, "Well—I'm only a stranger here, and I ain't got no frog —but if I had a frog I'd bet you."

And then Greeley says, "That's all right—that's all right— if you'll hold my box a minute I'll go and get you a frog;" and so the feller took the box, and put up his forty dollars along with Greeley's, and set down to wait.

So he set there a good while thinking and thinking to himself, and then he got the frog out and prized his mouth open and took a teaspoon and filled him full of quail-shot—filled him pretty near up to his chin—and set him on the floor. Greeley he went to the swamp and slopped around in the mud for a long time, and finally he ketched a frog and fetched him in and give him to this feller and says:

"Now if you're ready, set him alongside of Dan'l, with his fore-paws just even with Dan'l's, and I'll give the word." Then he says, "one—two—three—jump!" and him and the feller touched up the frogs from behind, and the new frog hopped off, but Dan'l give a heave, and hysted up his shoulders—so—like a Frenchman, but it wa'nt no use—he couldn't budge; he was planted as solid as an anvil, and he couldn't no more stir than if he was anchored out. Greeley was a good deal surprised, and he was disgusted, too, but he didn't have no idea what the matter was, of course.

The feller took the money and started away, and when he was going out at the door he sorter jerked his thumb over his shoulders—this way—at Dan'l, and says again, very deliberate: "Well—*I* don't see no points about that frog that's any better'n any other frog."

Greeley he stood scratching his head and looking down at Dan'l a long time, and at last he says, "I do wonder what in the nation that frog throw'd off for—I wonder if there ain't something the matter with him—he 'pears to look mighty baggy, somehow," and he ketched Dan'l by the nap of the neck, and lifted him up and says, "Why blame my cats if he don't weigh five pound," and turned him upside down, and he belched out about a double-handful of shot. And then he see how it was, and he was the maddest man—he set the frog down and took out after that feller, but he never ketched him. And—

[Here Simon Wheeler heard his name called from the front-yard, and got up to see what was wanted.] And turning to me as he moved away, he said: "Just set where you are, stranger, and rest easy—I ain't going to be gone a second."

But by your leave, I did not think that a continuation of

the history of the enterprising vagabond Jim Greeley would be likely to afford me much information concerning the Rev. Leonidas W. Greeley, and so I started away.

At the door I met the sociable Wheeler returning, and he buttonholed me and recommenced:

"Well, thish-yer Greeley had a yaller one-eyed cow that didn't have no tail only just a short stump like a bannanner, and—"

"O, curse Greeley and his afflicted cow!" I muttered, good-naturedly, and bidding the old gentleman good-day, I departed.

Yours, truly,   MARK TWAIN.

CALIFORNIAN, *December* 16, 1865.

CHAPTER XIV

𝕿𝖍𝖊 𝕮𝖍𝖗𝖎𝖘𝖙𝖒𝖆𝖘 𝕱𝖎𝖗𝖊𝖘𝖎𝖉𝖊

FOR GOOD LITTLE GIRLS AND BOYS

BY GRANDFATHER TWAIN

THE STORY OF A BAD LITTLE BOY THAT BORE A CHARMED LIFE

NCE there was a bad little boy, whose name was Jim—though, if you will notice, you will find that bad little boys are nearly always called James in your Sunday-school books. It was very strange, but still it was true, that this one was called Jim.

He didn't have any sick mother, either—a sick mother who was pious and had the consumption, and would be glad to lie down in the grave and be at rest, but for the strong love she bore her boy, and the anxiety she felt that the world would be harsh and cold toward him when she was gone. Most bad boys in the Sunday books are named James, and have sick mothers who teach them to say, "Now, I lay me down," etc. and sing them to sleep with sweet plaintive voices, and then kiss them good-night, and kneel down by the bedside and weep. But it was different with this fellow. He was named Jim, and there wasn't anything the matter with his mother— no consumption, or any thing of that kind. She was rather stout than otherwise, and she was not pious; moreover, she was not anxious on Jim's account; she said if he were to break his neck, it wouldn't be much loss; she always spanked Jim to sleep, and she never kissed him good-night; on the contrary, she boxed his ears when she was ready to leave him.

This is the first printing of this story with this title.—EDITOR.

Once, this little bad boy stole the key of the pantry and slipped in there and helped himself to some jam, and filled up the vessel with tar, so that his mother would never know the difference; but all at once a terrible feeling didn't come over him, and something didn't seem to whisper to him, "Is it right to disobey my mother? Isn't it sinful to do this? Where do bad little boys go who gobble up their good kind mother's jam?" and then he didn't kneel down all alone and promise never to be wicked any more, and rise up with a light, happy heart, and go and tell his mother all about it and beg her forgiveness, and be blessed by her with tears of pride and thankfulness in her eyes. No; that is the way with all other bad boys in the books, but it happened otherwise with this Jim, strangely enough. He ate that jam, and said it was bully, in his sinful, vulgar way; and he put in the tar, and said that was bully also, and laughed, and observed that "the old woman would get up and snort" when she found it out; and when she did find it out he denied knowing anything about it, and she whipped him severely, and he did the crying himself. Everything about this boy was curious—everything turned out differently with him from the way it does to the bad Jameses in the books.

Once he climbed up in Farmer Acorn's apple tree to steal apples, and the limb didn't break and he didn't fall and break his arm, and get torn by the farmer's great dog, and then languish on a sick bed for weeks and repent and become good. Oh, no—he stole as many apples as he wanted, and came down all right, and he was all ready for the dog, too, and knocked him endways with a rock when he came to tear him. It was very strange—nothing like it ever happened in those mild little books with marbled backs, and with pictures in them of men with swallow-tailed coats and bell-crowned hats and pantaloons that are short in the legs, and women with the waists of their dresses under their arms and no hoops on. Nothing like it in any of the Sunday-school books.

Once he stole the teacher's penknife, and when he was

afraid it would be found out and he would get whipped, he
slipped it into George Wilson's cap—poor Widow Wilson's
son, the moral boy, the good little boy of the village, who
always obeyed his mother, and never told an untruth, and
was fond of his lessons and infatuated with Sunday-school.
And when the knife dropped from the cap and poor George
hung his head and blushed, as if in conscious guilt, and the
grieved teacher charged the theft upon him, and was just in
the very act of bringing the switch down upon his trembling
shoulders, a white-haired improbable justice of the peace did
not suddenly appear in their midst and strike an attitude and
say, "Spare this noble boy—there stands the cowering cul-
prit! I was passing the school door at recess, and, unseen myself, I saw the theft committed!" And then Jim didn't get
whaled, and the venerable justice didn't read the tearful
school a homily, and take George by the hand and say such a
boy deserved to be exalted, and then tell him to come and
make his home with him, and sweep out the office, and make
fires, and run errands, and chop wood, and study law, and
help his wife to do household labors, and have all the balance
of the time to play, and get forty cents a month, and be
happy. No, it would have happened that way in the books,
but it didn't happen that way to Jim. No meddling old clam
of a justice dropped in to make trouble, and so the model boy
George got threshed, and Jim was glad of it. Because, you
know, Jim hated moral boys. Jim said he was "down on them
milksops." Such was the coarse language of this bad, neglected boy.

But the strangest things that ever happened to Jim was the
time he went boating on Sunday and didn't get drowned, and
that other time that he got caught out in the storm when he
was fishing on Sunday, and didn't get struck by lightning.
Why, you might look, and look, and look through the Sunday-school books, from now till next Christmas, and you
would never come across anything like this. Oh, no—you
would find that all the bad boys who go boating on Sunday

invariably get drowned, and all the bad boys who get caught out in storms, when they are fishing on Sunday, infallibly get struck by lightning. Boats with bad boys in them always upset on Sunday, and it always storms when bad boys go fishing on the Sabbath. How this Jim ever escaped is a mystery to me.

This Jim bore a charmed life—that must have been the way of it. Nothing could hurt him. He even gave the elephant in the menagerie a plug of tobacco, and the elephant didn't knock the top of his head off with his trunk. He browsed around the cupboard after essence of peppermint, and didn't make a mistake and drink aqua fortis. He stole his father's gun and went hunting on the Sabbath, and didn't shoot three or four of his fingers off. He struck his little sister on the temple with his fist when he was angry, and she didn't linger in pain through long summer days and die with sweet words of forgiveness upon her lips that redoubled the anguish of his breaking heart. No—she got over it. He ran off and went to sea at last, and didn't come back and find himself sad and alone in the world, his loved ones sleeping in the quiet churchyard, and the vine-embowered home of his boyhood tumbled down and gone to decay. Ah, no—he came home drunk as a piper, and got into the station house the first thing.

And he grew up, and married, and raised a large family, and brained them all with an axe one night, and got wealthy by all manner of cheating and rascality, and now he is the infernalist wickedest scoundrel in his native village, and is universally respected, and belongs to the Legislature.

So you see there never was a bad James in the Sunday-school books that had such a streak of luck as this sinful Jim with the charmed life.   MARK TWAIN.

CALIFORNIAN, *December 23, 1865.*

CHAPTER XV

Enigma

I AM COMPOSED of sixteen or seventeen letters.

My 16, 14, 3, 4, 6, 9, 15, is something or other, in a general way.

My 2, 11, 7, 14, is something else.

My 9, 6, 4, 10, 15, 11, is the other thing.

My 6, 16, 8, 14, 9, 3, 2, 1, 11, is most anything.

My 5, 3, 9, 14, 7, 3, 1, 11, 5, 6, 16, 2, 13, is most anything else.

My 4, 2, 16, 9, is a good deal like some of the things referred to above, though in what respect it has baffled even me to determine.

My 9, 3, 8, 12, is—is—well, I suppose it *is*, although I cannot see why.

Now, if anybody can cipher out that enigma, he is an abler man than I am, notwithstanding I got it up myself. It would be a real favor if some one would try, however. I have figured at it, and worked at it, and sweated over it, until I am disgusted, and *I* can make neither head nor tail of it. I thought it was rather neat at first, but I do not like it so well, now that I can't find out the answer to it. It looks rather easy at a first glance, but you will notice that the further you get into it the more it widens out.

This is my first effort in the enigma line, and, to speak the plain truth, I am considerably stunned at my own success. I do not seem to have just got the hang of this sort of thing, somehow. But I offer the entertaining little trifle to your readers for what it is worth—it may serve to amuse an idle year—and it cannot do much harm—it cannot more than drive a man mad, and make him massacre his relations.

MARK TWAIN.

CALIFORNIAN, *December 23, 1865.*

CHAPTER XVI

On Linden, Etc.

AND SPEAKING of steamboats reminds me of an incident of my late trip to Sacramento. I want to publish it as showing how going north on the river gradually enfeebles one's mind, and accounts for the strange imbecility of legislators who leave here sensible men, and become the reverse, to the astonishment of their constituents, by the time they reach their seats in the Capitol at Sacramento. John Paul, Lieutenant Ellis, and myself went up with Captain Poole to his room on the *Antelope* at ten o'clock last Saturday night, and by way of amusement, John Paul instituted an intellectual game. He recited the first line of "Hohenlinden:"

"On Linden, when the sun was low,"

I recited the second:

"All bloodless lay th' untrodden snow,"

Lieutenant Ellis the third:

"And dark as winter was the flow"

John Paul the fourth:

"Of Iser, rolling rapidly."

Lieutenant Ellis began the next verse, and we went through it regularly, as before.

Bill Stevenson was umpire. He held the watch, allowed a man ten seconds to recollect his line, and if he couldn't, called "Time!" and "passed the deal" to the next, and the delinquent had to send for the whisky. Or if a man misquoted a word, Bill checked the mistake on his memorandum, and it was good for four drinks. Well, we went clear through the whole poem, and only one mistake, of a single little word, was made. The drinks were ordered. We went through it again; result, one mistake, and the drinks. We went through it again; result, one mistake, and whisky. We repeated the operation; result, three misquotations, and three whiskies all round. We stayed with that poem all the way to Sacramento, arriving there at 3 in the morning, and here is the way the first verse of "Hohenlinden" stood the last time we recited it:

Myself—"On London when the tray was low—"
John Paul—"The curfew tolled the knell of parting day;"
Lieut. Ellis—"This world is but a fleeting show—"
Myself—("Hic!) Berrer dog'n ole dog Tray!"

Bill Stevenson said: "Texas, bring four quarts of whisky and charge to these gentlemen—such stupidity as this must be severely punished."

Now just see the effect that travelling in a northerly direction has on a man. The further you go the more idiotic you become. I don't wonder that those legislators give such frequent evidences of decaying intellect. Most of them go north, you know.   MARK TWAIN.

CALIFORNIAN, *April* 7, 1866.

CHAPTER XVII

The Moral Phenomenon

FARALLONES, August 20, 1866.

Publishers Californian:

GENTLEMEN:—You had better hire me to fill the vacant editorship of THE CALIFORNIAN. What you want is a good Moral tone to the paper. If I have got a strong suit, that is it. If I am a wild enthusiast on any subject, that is the one. I am peculiarly fitted for such a position. I have been a missionary to the Sandwich Islands, and I have got the hang of all that sort of thing to a fraction. I gave such excellent satisfaction in Hawaii nei that they let me off when my time was up. I was justly considered to be the high chief of that Serious Family down there. I mention here—and I mention it modestly—I mention it with that fatal modesty which has always kept me down—that the missionaries always spoke of me as the Moral Phenomenon when I was down there. They were amazed to behold to what a dizzy altitude human morality may be hoisted up, as exemplified in me. I am honestly proud of the title they have conferred upon me, and shall always wear it in remembrance of my brief but gratifying missionary labors in the Islands.

What you want is Morality. You have run too much poetry; you have slathered—so to speak—(missionary term,) —you have slathered too many frivolous sentimental tales into your paper; too much wicked wit and too much demoralizing humor; too much harmful elevating literature. What the people are suffering for, is Morality. Turn them over to me. Give me room according to my strength. I can fetch them!

Let me hear from you. You could not do better than hire

me. I can bring your paper right up. You ought to know, yourself, that when I play my hand in the high moral line, I take a trick every time.

Yours,   "MARK TWAIN."

Surnamed THE MORAL PHENOMENON.

CALIFORNIAN, *August 25,* 1866.

CHAPTER XVIII

Some Fair Hits

T HE first notice of Mark Twain's "Jumping Frog" that appeared in this journal, contains an allusion to Mr. Webb, "editor" of the volume, and to the necessity and value of his editorial services, which was certainly rather ungracious under the circumstances, and which we regretted upon reflection. In the light of the following explanation of the services actually rendered by Mr. Webb, which we find in the New York *Citizen*, we feel constrained to admit that our comment was not only ungracious, but unjust:

"The San Francisco *Californian* thinks that Mr. C. H. Webb's preface to the 'Jumping Frog' edited and published by him—though the *Californian* calls it 'Mark Twain's elegant volume'— is 'unnecessary to introduce the author to a Californian public.' Perhaps to a *Californian* public, but certainly not to the *American* public. And it must be borne in mind that books are not specially published for the Californian public, that public being the poorest in the world for buying books. Of its 'favorite and popular humorist' it called for only two hundred copies! 'Mark Twain' was in reality very little known in this parish, outside of a newspaper few, until the appearance of this volume. His 'book' in the form in which he had prepared it, was refused on all sides. Mr. Webb undertook to publish it mainly to introduce his friend to the public of this coast, and insure him an audience as a lecturer. With that view, the preface or 'advertisement' was written, and certainly Mr. 'Twain' is very much indebted to 'John

Paul' for his skill displayed in editing, the taste with which the volume is gotten up, and the 'prefatory advertisement.' Especially for the latter, since 'John Paul' therein stretches the truth to say that his author never descends to coarseness, when the reverse is essentially true. What the book would have been without judicious excision, the reader can very well judge. As it is, Mr. Webb incurred the expense and assumed the risk—and the book has not paid.

The *Californian*, which Mr. Webb founded and conducted to a success, omitting all mention of him as publisher and credit for the really handsome volume, turns round and takes an ill-natured shy at him for introducing its 'popular and favorite humorist' to a strange public, with a few words of somewhat extravagant praise. Truly, the Republic of Letters is ungrateful—that of California particularly so."

Though we have thought it proper to give the explanation, or rather the rebuke, of Mr. Webb's champion in his own words, and though we are not disposed to take exception to any part of it on our own account, we cannot say that we quite like its tone and spirit toward "Mark" himself. We do not remember anything that appears to us like "extravagant praise," in Mr. Webb's introduction of his friend to the "strange public." As to the alleged "coarseness," of the Californian humorist, that is a question, the decision of which would depend a great deal upon definitions, and might ultimately resolve itself into a question of taste. The canons by which it is to be decided, are as unsettled and confused, as those by which it was recently sought to test the morality of Mr. Swinburne's poems. We know of no satisfactory dogmas by which questions of this kind can be set at rest. So far as our own taste is concerned, while recognizing that "Mark Twain's" humor is of quite a different strain from Frank Bret Harte's for instance, we think we could find a better and more accurate term than "coarse" by which to characterize it. Indeed, such are the resources of the English language that we even believe that a tolerably discriminating notice of "Miles

O'Reilly" himself, as a humorist, might be written without pressing the objectionable adjective into the service. "What the book would have been without judicious excision," says the *Citizen*, "the reader can very well judge." How the reader is to judge what the book would have been without excision, or how he is to judge whether the excision was "judicious," in the absence of any knowledge of the matter which was removed by that surgical operation, we profess to be quite at a loss to understand. These remarks are not made with any wish to disparage the value of the services rendered by "John Paul" in editing his friend's book; much less are they prompted by any feeling of soreness resulting from the perfectly fair hit we have ourselves received. The only feature in the *Citizen's* mode of referring to the matter that impresses us disagreeably, is the somewhat patronizing attitude in which it places Mr. Webb with reference to his friend, an attitude which we are quite sure Mr. Webb himself would be the last to assume.

CALIFORNIAN, *August* 24, 1867

WICKED MARK TWAIN

It is just as we feared. Mark Twain was not the sort of man to be sent to the Holy Land. He tries to write in a Christian-like spirit, but as the only Christianity of which he had any experience is that of a Mississippi pilot (a very inferior article), it is not to be wondered at that, in his letters to the New York *Tribune*, he talks in a very irreverent Mississippi manner about sacred things and places. When we heard that Beecher was not going on the vessel which started with the pilgrims for the Holy Land, we felt inclined to telegraph to the managers of the speculation, and beg them to keep Mark Twain off the boat. Beecher might possibly have toned him down a little, but without any religious element to counteract the effects of this reckless joker's influence, we feared that the Holy Land pilgrims would become thoroughly demoralized by this licensed libertine. We will not republish the wicked things that Mark Twain says—we are surprised that the *Tribune* did not cut out some of them—we are glad, however, that he is back in New York. Mark Twain in the Holy Land was about as misplaced as an Ethiopian minstrel would be in a church choir.

CALIFORNIAN, *December* 7, 1867

MARK TWAIN.—Mark Twain is probably by this time in the Holy Land. Mark will first direct his steps to the spot rendered to him sacred by association with Ananias, an individual whose regard for veracity was fully equal to that of Mark himself. It is not unlikely that Ananias' shade will accompany Mark throughout his wanderings, a mutual, beautiful, and natural sympathy being established between them, more particularly arising from Mark's efforts to re-popularize Ananias about a year and a half ago, when he introduced him to the San Francisco public, as engaged in the business of swapping lies with Fitz-Smythe, on the outskirts of hell.

CALIFORNIAN, *August* 31, 1867

MARSH'S MANUAL

OF

Reformed Phonetic Short-Hand:

BEING A

COMPLETE GUIDE TO THE BEST SYSTEM

OF

PHONOGRAPHY AND VERBATIM REPORTING.

BY

ANDREW J. MARSH,

OFFICIAL REPORTER FOR THE COURTS.

———◆———

SAN FRANCISCO:
H. H. BANCROFT & COMPANY.
1868.

WOMAN.

["**Mark Twain's**" speech, in reply to the toast to "Woman," at the Correspondents' Club dinner, Washington, December, 1867.]

Mr. President,—I do not know why I should have received the greatest distinction of the evening, for so the office of replying to the toast of "Woman" has been regarded in every age. [Applause.] I do not know why such an honor should have been conferred upon me, unless it be that I am a trifle less homely than the other members of the club. But be this as it may, Mr. President, I am proud of the position, and you could not have chosen [1] any one who would have accepted it more gladly, or labored with a heartier good will to do the subject justice than I, because, sir, I love the sex; I love all women, sir, irrespective of age or color. [Laughter.] Human intelligence cannot estimate what we owe to woman, sir. She sews on our buttons; she mends our clothes. [Great laughter.] She ropes us in at the church fairs; she confides in us; she tells us whatever she can find out about the little private affairs of the neighbors. [Renewed laughter.] She gives us advice, and plenty of it.[2] She gives us a piece of her mind, sometimes, and sometimes all of it. [Laughter.] Wheresoever you place woman, sir, in whatever position or estate, she is an ornament to that place which she occupies, and a treasure to the world. [Here the speaker pauses, looking around upon his auditors inquiringly.] The applause ought to come in at this point. [Great laughter and applause.] Look at the noble names of history. Look at Cleopatra; look at Desdemona; look at Florence Nightingale; look at Joan of Arc; look at Lucretia Borgia. [Voices, "No, no!" The speaker pauses as if in some doubt.] Well, suppose we let Lucretia slide. [Laughter.] Look at Joyce Heth; look at Mother Eve. [Cries of "Oh! oh!" and laughter.] You need not look at her unless you want to. [Pauses reflectively.] But Eve was an ornament, sir, particularly before the fashions changed. [Renewed laughter.] I repeat, sir, look at the illustrious names of history. Look at the Widow Macree; look at Lucy Stone; look at Elizabeth Cady Stanton; look at Frances——Frances——George Francis Train. [Great laughter.] And, sir—I say it with bowed head, and deepest veneration—look at the mother of Washington. She raised a boy that couldn't lie—couldn't lie! [Applause.] It might have been otherwise with him if he had belonged to a newspaper correspondents' club. [Groans, hisses, cries of "Put him out," and laughter. The speaker placidly looks on until the seeming excitement subsides.] I repeat, sir, that in whatsoever

---

[1] "*And you could not have chosen.*" See §55.

[2] "*And plenty of it.*" "Of it," "of the," "have it," etc., are frequently added by the half-length and *cf*-hook, as "out of it (the)" "much of it," etc., on the same principle as that on which "not" is represented by a half-length stem and an *en*-hook. See last sentence in § 79.

position you place woman, she is an ornament to society, and a treasure
to the world. As a sweetheart, she has few equals, and no superiors.
[Great laughter.] As a cousin she is convenient. As a wealthy grand-
mother, with an incurable distemper, she is unspeakably precious.
What would the peoples of the earth be without woman? They would
be scarce, sir—fearfully scarce. [Renewed laughter.] Then let us cherish her; let us protect her; let us give her our support, our encour-
agement, our sympathy, ourselves, if we get a chance. [Laughter.]
But, jesting aside, Mr. President, woman is lovable, gracious, kind of
heart, beautiful, worthy of all respect, of all esteem, of all deference.
Not any here will refuse to drink her health right cordially, in this goblet
of wine, for each and every one of us has personally known, loved, and
honored the best of them all, his own mother. [Great applause.]

This amusing speech of Mark Twain's given at the
Correspondents' Club dinner, 1867, was first published in book form as a shorthand exercise. It was the
second article of Mark Twain's to appear in a book,
but being buried in such a curious out-of-the-way
place it was unknown to collectors until 1922 when it
was brought to my attention by a friend. It had appeared in Mark Twain's collected speeches of 1910,
but this version has many differences from the earlier
speech. The original text which I am reprinting in
exact facsimile has never appeared in any of Mark
Twain's collected works.—EDITOR.

NEW MERCANTILE LIBRARY,
BUSH STREET.

Thursday Evening, July 2, 1868.

ONE NIGHT ONLY.

FAREWELL LECTURE OF

MARK TWAIN.

SUBJECT:
The Oldest of the Republics, VENICE,
Past and Present.

Box Office open Wednesday and Thursday.

NO EXTRA CHARGE FOR RESERVED SEATS.

ADMISSION, - - - - - ONE DOLLAR.

Doors open at 7. Orgies to commence at 8 p. m.

☞ The public displays and ceremonies projected to give fitting eclat to this occasion, have been unavoidably delayed until the 4th. The lecture will be delivered certainly on the 2d, and the event will be celebrated two days afterward by a discharge of artillery on the 4th, a procession of citizens, the reading of the Declaration of Independence, and by a gorgeous display of fire-works from Russian Hill in the evening, which I have ordered at my sole expense, the cost amounting to eighty thousand dollars.

AT NEW MERCANTILE LIBRARY, BUSH ST.
Thursday Evening, July 2, 1868.

NEEDLESS TO SAY, THE LECTURE WAS WELL-ATTENDED

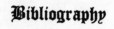

Bibliography

Bibliography

BRET HARTE MATERIAL FROM THE CALIFORNIAN
INCLUDING REVIEWS AND NOTICES
VOLUME I

VOLUME IV

° Reprint from *Territorial Enterprise.*
* Reprint from *New York Review.*
† Reprint from *New York Saturday Press.*
‡ Reprint from *Sacramento Union*

° Reprint from *Territorial Enterprise.*
* Reprint from *New York Review.*
† Reprint from *New York Saturday Press.*
‡ Reprint from *Sacramento Union.*